PICHAI

THE FUTURE OF GOOGLE

Jagmohan S. Bhanver has worked with three of the largest banks in India, handling national and international roles. Presently, he is an executive coach to CEOs and board members of various organizations. Bhanver's seminars on leadership and motivation have had a powerful impact on several lives and careers.

Bhanver is the author of three bestselling non-fiction titles and his first fiction title has recently been declared a national bestseller in India. He has also written for several TV shows and is in the process of finalizing a movie script. This is his fourth book of non-fiction. He can be found on Twitter at @authorjagmohan.

Also by the same author

Nadella: The Changing Face of Microsoft

PICHAI

THE FUTURE OF GOOGLE

Jagmohan S. Bhanver

First published in 2016 by Hachette India
(Registered name: Hachette Book Publishing India Pvt. Ltd)
An Hachette UK company
www.hachetteindia.com

1

ISBN 978-93-5195-061-5

Hachette Book Publishing India Pvt. Ltd
4th/5th Floors, Corporate Centre,
Sector 44, Gurgaon 122003, India

Typeset in Sabon 10.5/15
by InoSoft Systems, Noida

Printed and bound in India by
Manipal Technologies Ltd, Manipal

CONTENTS

INTRODUCTION

Over the past few months, since the appointment of the third chief executive officer (CEO) of IT giant Google on 10 August 2015, both the media and analysts have been speculating about the changes Sundar Pichai will bring about at Google. Needless to say, the kind of expectation that has stemmed from Pichai's appointment is unprecedented, and perhaps surpasses even that of Satya Nadella, when he was chosen to lead the world's fourth-largest company, Microsoft, just a year ago.

Unlike Microsoft and several other large technology companies, Google hasn't made too many mistakes in the past. This is not to say that it has been smooth sailing for Google so far, as they have faced fierce competition from Amazon, Microsoft, Apple and various other companies on different fronts. However, most of Google's recent product stories have been written right, and observers would be hard put to find fault with too many of them. In fact, Pichai's ability to come up with winning products has been something Google's co-founder Larry Page has lauded in the past. Now that the man behind most of those products is actually in the driver's seat, it will be interesting to see in which direction he plans to steer Google. On the flip side, there have been people who have criticized Google for going slow on innovation in recent years. Larry Page's decision to create Alphabet as the holding company and focus on moon shots through the newly formed entity may actually be a move to counter that criticism. It leaves Pichai to focus on making Google better at what it does. A leaner Google will also innovate better.

Sundar Pichai has been at the forefront of most of these developments, and with his promotion a lot of people will be keenly watching the developments at Google's Mountain View headquarters in California, USA. Google, under Sergey Brin, Eric Schmidt and Larry Page, has made huge strides since its beginning in 1998. Will the company lead the world into the next phase of technological innovation? More importantly, will Sundar Pichai be the man to take the company there?

Like Nadella, Sundar Pichai has not been much of

a public figure in the past. Very little is known of the man from Chennai who has rapidly risen through the ranks of the tech giant. What goads this man to excel? What does Pichai's appointment portend for Google and, possibly, for the tech industry as a whole?

In endeavouring to glean answers to these questions and several more, I have had the fortune of analysing not just Google but also its latest CEO. By all accounts, it appears that Google is set for a very interesting ride and Sundar Pichai may end up surprising his supporters and detractors alike.

Pichai's appointment as CEO of Google and Larry Page's transition to Alphabet is merely the tip of the iceberg. The actual story of Google's new innings will start unfurling over the following months and will continue for at least a couple of years from now. By all accounts, Google appears to be in safe hands. However, only time will tell whether Google will supersede its biggest rivals or end up losing its current market share to more nimble players. In the interim, this book attempts to give an insight into Sundar Pichai, the man and the professional, and what his recent promotion means for Google, and for the future of technology.

PART 1

THE DREAMER

'The thing that attracted me to Google and to the Internet in general is that it's a great equalizer. I want Google to strive to do that; not just build technology for certain segments. For me, it matters that we drive technology as an equalizing force, as an enabler for everyone around the world.'

– Sundar Pichai

The inception of an idea

'Life has no limitations, except the ones you make.'

– Les Brown

The Mobile World Congress (MWC) today is veritably the largest exposition for the mobile industry, where heads of various mobile operators, technology providers, manufacturers and content owners meet to talk about the latest innovations and happenings in the mobile world, and the impact this will have on mobile users all over the globe. The 2015 Mobile World Congress in Barcelona was no exception. In fact, it was the largest gathering in the history of the exhibition. Imagine 94,000 participants from more than 2,000 organizations and 200 countries, all in one place!

What marked this particular event though was not just the significant number of attendees, but also the speech given by a Google representative, introduced by Brad Stone of *Bloomberg Business Week*. Interestingly, Brad Stone, in a June 2014 article in his magazine, had referred to this very person as 'the most powerful man in mobile'. The man was none other than Sundar Pichai, then senior vice-president at Google, and now the CEO of the legendary company.

The thousands of people gathered at the MWC in Barcelona, listening with bated breath to Pichai's dreams and plans of a 'mobile Google', might be forgiven for not knowing that the speaker's story began in a place called Ashok Nagar in Chennai, where, 30 years ago, a 12-year-old Sundar Pichai held a rotary phone in his young hands for the very first time. It was the first phone his family had ever owned!

It was perhaps right then that the possibilities of what a phone could do flooded Sundar's mind. While it may be conjecture, one feels compelled to surmise that his love for technology and its unlimited power to make positive changes for people everywhere, may have germinated within his being in that very moment.

The early years

'Difficulties are meant to rouse, not discourage. The human spirit is to grow strong by conflict.'

– William Ellery Channing

Most people who have succeeded in their lives have had their fair share of challenges. If everyone who won the race had a favoured past, there would be no motivational stories to inspire those who haven't had fortune shine upon them yet. One thing that separates the true winners from the also-rans is their indomitable spirit to rise above their tribulations and go to war with whatever they have, rather than sit at home complaining about what they don't.

Sundar Pichai belongs to the tribe of achievers, and Channing's words never rang as true as they appear to do in his case. Born on 12 July 1972, in Madurai, Pichai's childhood was spent in Chennai. While the

Pichai family was not impecunious, their coffers were certainly not overflowing with riches either. Sundar's father, Regunatha, was employed as a senior engineer with a British multinational company that made switchgears. Lakshmi, his mother, worked as a stenographer but gave up her job after Sundar and his brother Sreenivasan were born. A traditional, down-to-earth family, the Pichais' focus was on ensuring that the children got the best education possible, which meant that comforts like a television set or a car had to be sacrificed. Their Chennai apartment boasted two rooms and this necessitated that Sundar and his brother sleep in the living room. Travel was restricted to the overcrowded public transport or riding shotgun with his father on their old Lambretta scooter while his younger brother brought up the pillion.

The Pichais' simple lifestyle helped keep the children grounded. Sundar's focus was on his studies, though in later years, during high school, cricket became an additional attraction and something he found himself faring rather well in. At this stage, Sundar's life was influenced by two very distinct experiences:

One, Regunatha shared with the boys stories of his workplace and the challenges he faced there. These anecdotes seemed to have a profound impact on Sundar. Even at that age, he appeared to be attracted to anything that had to do with technology, possibly sowing the seeds of innovation in his growing mind.

Secondly, holding the family's first phone in his hands did more than just attract him to technology. It made him think of the unlimited power technology could wield to change the life of the common man. On a different note, it also revealed an extraordinary gift he had not known he had – Sundar Pichai found he had an uncanny ability to remember any number that he had ever dialled!

Competition begins at school

> *'My father and mother did what a considerable measure of parents did at the time. They sacrificed a considerable measure of their life and utilized a great deal of their extra cash to verify their kids were educated.'*
>
> – Sundar Pichai

The first phase of what is now popularly referred to as Pichai's 'self-driven' attitude kicked off at Jawahar Vidyalaya School in Ashok Nagar, Chennai. While Jawahar Vidyalaya is considered among the good schools in Chennai, it is certainly not in the league of top schools across the country. Yet, there must have been something in the school's ethos and in young

Pichai's inherent nature that would propel him to go for success. It's interesting that the man who was able to grab the attention of Google founders Larry Page and Sergey Brin was quite inconspicuous during his school days. Not too many of the faculty from Jawahar Vidyalaya or the other school he studied at – Vana Vani Matriculation Higher Secondary School – remember Pichai very clearly. R.M. Krishnan, who was the principal of Jawahar Vidyalaya, joked that professors tend to remember either the top students or the naughty ones. Sundar was an intelligent boy, but a quiet one nevertheless.

After completing his 10th grade from Jawahar Vidyalaya, Sundar moved to Vana Vani, which is located inside the IIT Chennai campus and is the breeding ground for a lot of future IIT-ians. Sundar was here for two years and completed his 12th grade under the Tamil Nadu state board curriculum in 1989.

Even as a student, the current CEO of Google set goals for himself. He demonstrated a degree of self-drive that is rare in one so young. Sundar's father has spoken several times about how he never had to tell Sundar to study because Sundar would be doing it on his own without being told. Sundar's friends also talk about his unwavering attention as he would read a book even in the cycle rickshaw on the way to school and back home.

In Chennai, Sundar represents the quintessence of what is known as the 'IIT boy'. And it wasn't any coincidence that he landed up at IIT Kharagpur after passing out of Vana Vani. While most kids his age were playing cricket or were preoccupied with other street games, Sundar would be sitting somewhere reading a book or studying. He was so fiercely competitive that he would fight even for a single mark and not rest until he had got it.

IIT boy

'Some people dream of success...while others wake up and work hard at it.'

– Winston Churchill

In 1946, two educationists, Humayun Kabir and Jogendra Singh, decided it would be easier to facilitate industrial development in India if the country had technical institutions built on the same framework as the famed Massachusetts Institute of Technology (MIT) in the USA. With the help of B.C. Roy, who became the chief minister of Bengal in 1948, they formed a committee headed by Nalini Ranjan Sarkar, which later on came to be known as the Sarkar Committee. Roy persuaded Prime Minister Jawaharlal Nehru about the need for such institutions in the country. Since there were many industries in West Bengal at the time, the first such institute was commenced in West Bengal itself. Thus, was born the first IIT in May 1950 and it was located at Esplanade East, Kolkata. Four months later, the institute moved to a place called Hilji in Midnapore district. This was an interesting choice as Hilji was formerly a detention camp for Indian freedom fighters. Now it was set to be the centre stage for the opening of an institute that would enable India to assert its independence in industrial growth.

Hilji is located beside Kharagpur, which was part of the 200-year-old Hilji kingdom that came to an end in 1886. It was not surprising, therefore, that the Indian Institute of Technology here was named IIT-Kharagpur. The institute commenced its session in August 1951 when it was inaugurated by Maulana Abul Kalam Azad. In September 1956, the Indian Parliament declared IIT-Kharagpur an institute of national importance. Nehru, at the first convocation of the institute, spoke eloquently, 'Here in the place of that Hilji detention camp, stands the fine monument of India, representing India's urges, India's future in the making. This picture seems to me symbolical of the changes that are coming to India'.[1]

It was at IIT Kharagpur's sprawling 2,100-acre

campus which Sundar Pichai joined in 1989, that he found himself rubbing shoulders with the people who would define technology not just in India but all over the world. He joined the metallurgical department that has produced other high achievers such as Praveen Chaudhari (director at the Brookhaven National Laboratory, USA and previously head of IBM's research division). Arun Sarin (who was CEO at Vodafone) was another product of Kharagpur's metallurgical division, as was Vinod Gupta, chairman of Everest Group LLC, a US-based venture capital and private equity firm.

Better known as P. Sundarajan during his stint at IIT, Sundar kept a relatively low profile though he was well respected by fellow students as well as professors. The boy from Nehru Hall (Sundar's hostel at Kharagpur) topped his batch from the word 'go'. This continued even during his final year in 1993 when he not only topped metallurgy, but was also given the institute's prestigious silver medal for academic excellence.

While Sundar was enrolled in the metallurgy programme, he was immensely interested in electronics, too. The suppleness of the IIT system encouraged Sundar to balance both his interest and his core curriculum. From his third year onwards, Sundar used IIT's platform to develop his knowledge on the behaviour of electronic materials. So much so that even his B. Tech thesis was on electronic materials.

Prof. Sanat Roy, who was one of Sundar's professors at Kharagpur says, 'He was doing work in the field of electronics at a time when no separate course on electronics existed in our curriculum. His thesis dealt with implanting molecules of other elements in silicon wafers to alter its properties. It was very clear from the beginning that he was enthused about electronics and materials.'[2]

At IIT, Sundar started showing signs of going beyond the 'bookish' aura he had created around himself during his school days in Chennai. His people skills and communication developed and he was able to forge strong relationships. At Nehru Hall itself, he had a close group of 14 friends whom he keeps in touch with even now. One of these hostel mates, Prashant Tripathy, who is currently director and CFO of Max Life Insurance, says, 'I found him sharp and articulate. When discussions took place within our group, he usually took centre stage. He was very friendly and helpful. Not at all the "nerdy guy" that one might assume. We used to watch movies till late night at times. These were times when the Internet wasn't there and most of our time was spent talking to friends. He also used to read a lot.'[3]

Sundar's stint at IIT got him more than a bunch of good friends and the institute's silver medal. This is also the place where he met the woman who would become his wife and life partner.

Romantic at heart

'The very essence of romance is uncertainty.'

– Oscar Wilde

If you thought making it to the post of the CEO at Google may have been tough for Sundar, close friends of Google's head honcho would probably disagree. Apparently, one of the biggest challenges Sundar ever faced was proposing to the woman he loved. In classic style, Sundar fell in love with a girl in the chemical engineering department from the same batch. She was from Kota, Rajasthan, while Sundar was from Tamil Nadu. He gave the relationship the same passion he brought to all other things in his life.

The girl who had Sundar Pichai besotted was Anjali Haryani. It was characteristic of Sundar that not even his closest friends knew about his interest in Anjali until after they had graduated from IIT. While Sundar proposed to her during their final year, they were able to marry only a few years later. After IIT, he went to the USA to do his Master of Science (MS) at Stanford. Unable to obtain a student loan, his father had to withdraw funds from the family's savings to pay for Sundar's flight and other miscellaneous expenses. It cost the elder Pichai a year's salary, but it put Sundar on the right track.

Stanford was followed by a stint at a Silicon Valley semiconductor firm, Applied Materials. It was a tough period for Sundar as he was unable to stay in touch with Anjali, sometimes for a period of six months at a stretch. This was a time when telecommunications in India were not too developed and international calling rates were prohibitively expensive.

It was only when Sundar joined Applied Materials that he asked his parents for their permission to marry Anjali. The Pichai family gave their consent and the young couple was finally bound in marriage. Subsequently, Anjali joined Sundar in the US. When Sundar joined McKinsey as a consultant, Anjali decided to follow in his footsteps and did an MS from Stanford, much like Sundar had done earlier. This time, of course, the circumstances were different – the two of them were together.

A man with a mind of his own

'Don't keep forever on the public road, going only where others have gone.'

– Alexander Graham Bell

While outwardly quiet and apparently easy-going, Sundar has a will of steel that surfaces when it is required to. He has time and again demonstrated that he will do what he believes in, and that he believes in what he does.

At IIT, he went against the tide when, despite being enrolled the metallurgical programme, he did a thesis in electronics at a time when no separate course on the subject existed at the institute. Later, his professors at IIT suggested that he undertake a PhD programme at Stanford, where he had earned a scholarship. Instead, Sundar dropped out of the PhD programme and did an MS in materials science and engineering.

Afterwards, while working for Applied Materials, he yet again decided to do things differently. Much to the initial chagrin of his parents, he quit the job and enrolled for an MBA at the Wharton School of Business. Here, he was named a Siebel Scholar and Palmer Scholar. The Siebel Scholars' programme essentially recognizes outstanding students from 27 graduate schools in the US, China, Japan, Italy and France. Apart from Wharton, it includes institutes like the MIT-Sloan Institute of Management, Kellogg School of Management, Stanford Graduate School of Business, Harvard Business School, Carnegie Mellon University, Princeton University and Johns Hopkins University. Every year, a Siebel Scholar is chosen from each of the institutions, based on the deans' recommendations. The winner gets an award of $35,000. The Palmer Scholar award is given to those students who graduate in the top five per cent of the class. The rank in class is calculated based on the student's cumulative grade point average (GPA) earned during the two-year stint at Wharton.

To an extent, Sundar's decision to do an MS in materials science and engineering from Stanford contributed greatly to his understanding of the business at Google and his ability to add value to the Google founders' own thought processes. Sundar is skilled at dealing with density, semiconductors, molecular mechanics and materials that make good semiconductors – essentially the building blocks of computers. On the other hand, Larry Page and Sergey Brin's outlook and qualifications are bent more towards the software side of the business. Pichai's expertise literally blends the software as well as the hardware story, which could be a terrific advantage for Google in the present technology environment.

Gully cricket

'Cricket to us was more than play; it was a worship in the summer sun.'

– Edmund Blunden

There is something about Indians and cricket that is literally inseparable.

Cricket is one thing where even the most diligent student would make a concession and watch a match or at least discuss its intricacies with their friends. Sundar Pichai is not an exception to this rule.

During his earlier years at school, however, he did not show much interest in discussing cricket. Sundar's grandmother Ranganayaki says that while Sundar (she calls him by his nickname, Rajesh) did not like wasting time, he and his younger brother Sreenivasan would play cricket in front of their house after school. Later, he was captain of his high school cricket team. At IIT Kharagpur, he was no different from the rest of his group at Nehru Hall, when it came to spending hours at night discussing the sport or dissecting a match they had seen recently.

It is interesting that Sundar's compatriot and another high-achieving Indian in the field of technology, Satya Nadella, CEO of Microsoft, also professes his love for cricket and what the sport has taught him about leadership.

Not an elitist

'Sundar Pichai is a metaphor for a new kind of elitism in the US.'

– Wajahat Qazi

Historically, any major event is followed by a plethora of salubrious and some not-so-wholesome reactions. Pichai's ascension as CEO of Google was not an exception. Among the not-so-favourable coverage was an article by Wajahat Qazi.[4]

While the article was not directly targeted at Pichai, it contained some pointed remarks that involved the new Google CEO and other talented Indians in the US. In the rather befuddled article, Qazi talks about a rising elite in the US (epitomized by Pichai) and how this has been instrumental in large measure in creating the angst faced by the working class white American. In his piece in Firstpost.com, Qazi seemed to imply that immigrants – mostly from India – going to the US had it easier than homegrown Americans who did not have the same access to mentoring, education and opportunities that the immigrants had. While some may tend to agree with his views, anyone will be compelled to wonder at the theory Qazi puts forth in the article. For instance, there are very few places today where opportunities for education and mentoring are as high as in the US, and people from developing nations certainly don't enjoy that advantage.

However, Qazi unwittingly does recognize that most of the so-called elites who have moved to the US have earned their stripes purely on merit; and nowhere is this more evident than in the case of Sundar Pichai, whom Qazi refers to as a metaphor for a new kind of elitism in the US! If Qazi had taken a little pain to delve into Pichai's background, he may have found that this is a man who didn't let the disadvantages of his youth decide the future course of his career; that here is a man who has struggled to compete with the best of the best in a nation that perhaps ranks the highest in the world on competitiveness but rather low on the spectrum of opportunities. In 1993, after landing in the US on a scholarship to Stanford, Pichai did not have enough money to buy a backpack for himself. When he heard that it cost $60, he was shocked. Surely, this cannot be the elitist and privileged man Qazi refers to in his article. The fact that Pichai's father had to dip into his savings to buy Sundar's flight tickets also fails to support the 'elitist' tag Qazi attributes so easily to Sundar and others of his ilk.

On the contrary, Sundar Pichai is a metaphor for a new kind of meritocratic global citizen; the type that ought to evoke pride not just within India but also within the country (the US) that has allowed him to succeed entirely by his accomplishments.

Just before Google

> *'Our mission is to help our clients make distinctive, lasting, and substantial improvements in their performance and to build a great firm that attracts, develops, excites, and retains exceptional people.'*
>
> – McKinsey

McKinsey was founded in 1926 by James McKinsey to apply accounting principles to management. Today, it is one of the most reputed management consulting firms in the world, the Galleon scandal notwithstanding.

Sundar joined McKinsey in 2001 at a time when another well-known Indian – Rajat Gupta – was at the helm of McKinsey's global operations as the first non-American in the role. Pichai worked at the consulting firm for three years before leaving for Google in 2004, a year after Rajat Gupta had been replaced by another McKinsey stalwart, Ian Davis.

It was while at McKinsey that he completed his MBA from the Wharton School of Business. While Applied Materials taught Sundar the intricacies of semiconductors, his stint at McKinsey helped him develop management skills that would later come in handy at Google. However, his engineering and business skills are a small part of what defines him as a leader. Somewhere along the way, Sundar Pichai picked up the kind of acumen that is rare to see even in much older and experienced leaders. Perhaps, the man from Chennai always had those skills within him and merely needed the right ecosystem for it to flourish – an ecosystem called Google!

[illegible] for three years before leaving for Google in 2004, [illegible] Rajat Gupta had been replaced by [illegible] McKinsey [illegible] Ian Davis.

It was while at McKinsey that he completed his MBA from the Wharton School of Business. [illegible] McKinsey [illegible] at Google [illegible] called Google!

PART 2

THE RISING STAR

'A key part of this (restructuring of Google and formation of Alphabet) is Sundar Pichai. Sundar has been saying the things I would have said (and sometimes better!) for quite some time now, and I've been tremendously enjoying our work together. He has really stepped up since October of last year, when he took on product and engineering responsibility for our Internet businesses. Sergey and I have been super excited about his progress and dedication to the company.'

– Larry Page

The changing landscape in the technology business

'In my opinion, all previous advances in the various lines of invention will appear totally

insignificant when compared with those which the present century will witness. I almost wish that I might live my life over again to see the wonders which are at the threshold.'

– Charles Holland Duell

Perhaps one of the most popular and misquoted statements of the century is attributed to Charles Duell, who was commissioner at the US Patent and Trademarks office between 1898 and 1901. In an apparent case of Chinese whispers, Duell has been misquoted as saying, 'Everything that could have been invented has been.' Ironically, this is not what the erstwhile commissioner said. If anything, his actual statement, made in 1902, (quoted above) reflected his excitement at the changes and discoveries he instinctively knew were on the way. This is borne out by the fact that the number of patents in the United States went up from 435 in 1837 to 25,527 in 1899. Duell knew the world was at the tipping point of discoveries and inventions that would make everything that had happened in the past look like a primary school science project.

The incredible 1990s

Duell's incredible foresight was borne out over the

ensuing years. The nineties, for instance, changed the way most of us looked at technology and its impact on people. In 1993, Microsoft introduced Windows NT that paved the way for MS-DOS and Windows. Apple Inc. came out with a Personal Digital Assistant (PDA), which was part of their Newton project. Both Microsoft and Apple would several years later prove to be two of the most formidable competitors for Google and, by extension, for Sundar Pichai.

In 1994, a man called Jeff Bezos left his job at a top investment firm on Wall Street, DE Shaw, and moved to Seattle to start his own company. Just four years prior to that he had been named the youngest VP at DE Shaw. DE Shaw's loss was a boon for the world as Bezos went on to found Amazon.com. Keen to maximize the opportunity offered by the Web, Bezos named his startup after the Amazon river. Bezos wanted Amazon to be the largest online store, and as exotic and different as the Amazon river. In 1997, Larry Page and Sergey Brin registered Google.com; in the same year Jeff Bezos issued Amazon's initial public offering (IPO) trading on the NASDAQ at a price of $18 per share. Today, Amazon is one of the major contenders that Google and Sundar Pichai need to consider when it comes to cloud computing services.

In August 1991, the World Wide Web became available publicly. While the World Wide Web had its foundation in work that Tim Berners-Lee did in the 1980s at CERN, the European organization for nuclear research, it was later extended into a far more comprehensive proposal recommending a World Wide Web of documents connected via hypertext links. In 1990, Berners-Lee was working on a computer built by NeXT, the firm Steve Jobs launched after exiting Apple in the mid-eighties. It was on a NeXT computer that Berners-Lee developed the first Web browser software and called it the World Wide Web. In 1993, CERN declared that it was free for everyone to use and develop. The first graphical web browser to become popular, Mosaic, inspired the first commercial browser, Netscape Navigator. At the same time, Mosaic's technology went on to form the basis of Microsoft's Internet Explorer. Several years later, Sundar Pichai from Google would take it upon himself to unseat the ruling browser and make Chrome the preferred choice for users.

In 1997, Larry and Sergey registered Google.com as a domain. The name they had chosen was inspired by 'googol', a mathematical term for the number represented by the numeral 'one' followed by a hundred zeros. The domain name expressed Larry Page and Sergey Brin's mission to organize an infinite amount of information on the web.

The amazing 2000s

2004 was a seminal year for both Sundar Pichai and the organization he would later head as CEO. Not just that, if anything, the first decade of the new millennium portended even more excitement for the entire technology industry than the previous decade had.

However, the beginning wasn't altogether great. In March 2000, the dotcom bubble climbed to a peak and reached a zenith of 5,132 on the NASDAQ. Shortly thereafter, the speculative bubble eventually burst, wiping out more than $5 trillion from the value of technology businesses. Hundreds of startups were wiped out and several blue-chip investors lost not just their funds but considerable face, too.

In 2001, Wikipedia was launched. Prior to this, the only online encyclopedia of note was Nupedia, started by Bomis – a web advertising company – and owned by Jimmy Wales, Tim Shell and Michael Davis. The editor-in-chief at Nupedia, Larry Sanger, convinced Wales and a few others at Nupedia to allow a new online encyclopedia (that he later called Wikipedia) to act as a feeder to Nupedia. The difference would be that unlike Nupedia, where the content was reviewed by expert editors, Wikipedia would be mostly self-regulated. Shortly thereafter, Wikipedia overtook

Nupedia. Today, its global readership per month exceeds half a billion, making it the world's seventh most popular website as far as visitor traffic to the site is concerned.

Advances in data compression in the 2000s involved encoding information using fewer bits than was done originally. Compression can take the form of either lossy or lossless – the former cuts down on bits by identifying unimportant information and taking it out while the latter reduces bits by removing statistical redundancy. In simple terms, the procedure of reducing the size of a data file is called data compression. When the data is transmitted, this is referred to as source coding which involves encoding at the source of the data prior to it being stored or transmitted. The advancement in data compression tied in with the surge in music downloading and coincided with the increase in sales of portable digital audio players. While this gave birth to a slew of MP3 players, a classic case was Apple's iPod which surfaced in November 2001. Given its storage capacity and the user-friendly interface, the iPod was an instant success. Apple's fortunes underwent a significant change with the introduction of the iTunes store as millions of customers lined up to download songs. By 2005, online music sales already accounted for six per cent of all music sales in the world. Subsequently, digital music options were integrated into devices like smartphones and the PSP (Play Station Portable) from Sony Corporation. Since then, data compression has defined the way ahead for several digital utilities and services, literally changing the landscape for all the technology players, including the big ones like Apple, Google, Amazon and Microsoft.

In the early 2000s, Flash was used to display web pages and online games. Enhancements in Flash technology enabled the making of video players. Consequently in 2005, the newly started YouTube used Flash Player to display compressed video content on the web. In 2007, YouTube offered videos in HTML5 format that supported Apple's iPhone and iPad but incidentally did not support Flash Player. In October 2006, Google bought YouTube for $1.65 billion in an all-stock deal amidst rumours that the latter had competed with Yahoo for the acquisition.

On the operating system (OS) front, Microsoft's Windows XP and Microsoft Office 2003 became a sort of industry standard. On the browser side, Microsoft's Internet Explorer ruled the roost even though the free and open source browser Firefox from Mozilla Corporation gave them a run for their money in certain parts of the world. In later years, Sundar Pichai realized that Google risked losing its primary source of revenue from Search if it remained dependent on Microsoft's Internet Explorer. While we cover this in greater detail in the following sections of the book, this realization prompted Pichai and Google to hasten work on their browser. The result was Google Chrome, a freeware web browser that was launched in September 2008. Google's operating system, Chrome OS was launched in July 2009 and in it the applications and user data both reside in the Cloud. It essentially means that within a few seconds of switching on your computer you could be connected to the Internet.

Very importantly, at this time, broadband Internet usage increased all over the world. In 2000, the usage was barely 6 per cent of the overall Internet usage in the US. By 2010, it had surpassed all expectations and jumped up to more than eighty per cent. In fact, broadband Internet was by then viewed as a norm for a high-quality Internet browsing experience. This obviously had implications for any player who wanted to make their presence felt in the Internet-enabled services space. Google, whose primary source of revenue came from Internet search, couldn't afford to ignore this trend. Neither could others like Microsoft or Amazon.

The other event that was meaningful during this period was the shift in broadband speeds. In the nineties, dial-up connections were the only way to access the Internet but in the 2000s, broadband became the technology of choice. While this trend commenced in the developed nations, it was rapidly copied by several other countries.

The threshold speed required to meet the broadband criterion is 4 Mbit/s. By 2014, the average connection speed at a global level was 4.6 Mbit/s. While the US clocked an average speed of 11.4 Mbit/s, places like South Korea and Hong Kong registered 24.6 Mbit/s and 15.7 Mbit/s respectively, becoming the top two in the world as far as broadband Internet speeds were concerned. UAE mirrored the global average at 4.6 Mbit/s and Uruguay came up at a surprising 5.6 Mbit/s. What is incredible is the fact that most countries have been experiencing a year on year growth of 25 to 50 per cent. The ramification of this on Internet-enabled businesses is not too hard to miss. It will also aid Google and Sundar Pichai's goal of making Search and other e-enabled services available to people across the world, irrespective of where they are or which social strata they belong to. Anyone who has a smart phone or a basic Internet-enabled laptop or desktop will be able to access the same information that a billionaire in the developed world or a professor sitting at Harvard would be able to.

In 2003, a phenomenon took place that changed the way people interacted with each other. This was the beginning of social media. Myspace.com, founded by Chris DeWolfe and Tom Anderson, was the largest social networking site in the world till 2008, when Facebook finally overtook it. The launch of Myspace.com was followed by Google coming out with Orkut in January 2004. The service was named after its creator, Orkut Buyukkokten, a Google employee. Orkut caught the world's attention, and was immensely popular in USA, Japan, Brazil and India. A month later, Mark Zuckerberg came up with Facebook which took the thunder away from Orkut and took the world by storm. By 2015, Facebook was ahead of eBay and Amazon and ranked lower than only three other American web companies – Google, Microsoft and Apple. It was also the fastest company in the S&P 500 Index to reach a market cap of $250 billion. Twitter, launched in 2006, became one of the widest used platforms to share information in real time. Founded by Evan Williams, Jack Dorsey, Noah Glass and Biz Stone, the company rapidly moved into the ranks of the top ten most visited websites in the world. Sites like LinkedIn, Pinterest, Tumblr and Flickr are among several others that helped fashion the social networking landscape. Today, the immense pull these websites exhibit has become a key opportunity for advertisers, and an incredible source of ad revenue for these sites. Therefore, it is not surprising that

Facebook or Twitter today compete with Google for a share in the large advertising pie. What has also been defined are the kind of applications and strategies that technology companies and even non-technology businesses will need to come up with if they want to take advantage of data thrown up by some of these sites.

Several other developments in the 2000s have had tremendous bearing on Google and its peers. The vastly changed landscape has presented both opportunities and challenges for leading players. No approach is guaranteed to succeed for too long as the rules of the game are evolving quicker than they ever have before. Companies that focus on collaboration and early adoption of new technologies and who are willing to reinvent themselves or re-model themselves either organically or through corporate actions will have a better chance at being successful.

It remains to be seen if Google under Sundar Pichai is able to do this, and who among the main contenders in the technology sector will ease into a clear number one slot, a place that thus far has eluded everyone, including the inhabitants of Googleplex.

Coming home to Google

'By prevailing over all obstacles and distractions, one may unfailingly arrive at his chosen goal or destination.'

– Christopher Columbus

It was 2004. Facebook and Orkut had already been launched when Sundar Pichai left McKinsey and joined Google as one of the countless managers in product management. As Columbus said, years of hard work and tiding over numerous obstacles and tribulations had eventually got Pichai to the place where he could set his dreams in motion.

Pichai's joining of Google coincided with the company launching a free email service called Gmail on 1 April 2004. He half believed the whole thing was a joke because the date is infamous as All Fools' Day. He was to realize he had been wrong when Gmail quickly overtook other popular email services. While initially Gmail commenced as a beta version, and for some time was used by internal employees of Google, it was made available publicly on an invitation-only basis in April 2004. Three years later, in February 2007, Gmail was opened up to the public at large. It was upgraded from beta status in April 2007. Gmail started off by providing 1 GB of free space to users at a time when peers like Yahoo and Hotmail offered a 2 MB storage capacity. It compelled competitors to offer considerably increased space to customers. Both Hotmail and Yahoo offered their Plus customers space of 2GB and 1 GB respectively. However, by and large most users of these two popular mail services still had to contend with only 100 to 250 MB of free storage. Gmail's entry into the mail services market did more than just push players into offering additional free space; it resulted in Yahoo and Hotmail enhancing their email interfaces as well. (In fact this is one area that is still considered to be a weakness for Gmail.) While there are enough loyalists for the latter, very few users doubt that Gmail can do with serious upgrades to its interface within the user's web browser. Be that as it may, a 2014 study suggested that 60 per cent of mid-sized organizations in the US were Gmail users. Even more significantly, in the same year, Gmail had the distinction of becoming the first app on Google Play Store to touch one billion installations on Android devices!

Interestingly, Gmail probably represents the first launch from Google that really got them in a soup. Up until the launch of Gmail, Larry Page and Sergey Brin had been able to excite almost everyone about all their products, the most notable one of course being Search. Gmail was a different story. Right in the beginning, the Google team knew they had a great product. While the initial users of Gmail were Google employees, a few 100 select users were subsequently given the opportunity to try out the new product. Later, these happy customers were allowed to give away a limited number of accounts to their family members and friends. It was a great way to beta test the product. Also, not making it available en masse to start with created just the right level of anticipation in the world at large.

And it would have been perfect had Google just launched Gmail and not tried to replicate the success of their 'text ad' model in the Search business in the case of Gmail too. Those who have followed Google's success would remember that Google was the only player in the Search business who did not flood their users with meaningless banner ads. Nor did they believe in allowing paying advertisers to get a say in where they would be listed. While Google adopted Overture Inc's model of putting small text ads alongside the search results, they veered away from what they considered Overture's unethical manner of giving prominence to paid businesses. It worked like a charm. Internet experts like Danny Sullivan commended them for their brave and ethical business model and users obviously loved the fact that Google was not cluttered with meaningless ads and that sponsored listings put up by Google were clearly mentioned as 'sponsored'. More importantly, the sponsored listings were linked to what the user was searching for in the first place and that made them truly relevant for the users. This was the beginning of millions in ad revenue coming to Google.

Yet, the savvy and customer-centric Google founders made a gargantuan mistake with Gmail. In a classic case of inside-out thinking, Google decided that what had worked for Search would also work for Mail. They decided to adopt a similar model of placing text ads on the right-hand side of Gmail. In order to benefit users and businesses, Google claimed they would be looking at contextual ads. Exactly what Google meant by this was announced by Wayne Rosing, Google's Vice President of Engineering, around the time of Gmail's launch. Rosing said in an interview, 'Gmail grew out of experiments that involved our ad targeting. We did some textual analysis and were able to make it work.'[5]

While the announcement did make players like Yahoo and MSN start to sweat, it had a lot of people including politicians and regular users up in arms. The implication that Google may be peeping inside their private mails to understand the context and then place contextually relevant ads was anathema to a lot of people. Google began to be compared to Big

Brother and all of a sudden, the youthful 'do no evil' brand was no longer the innocent player it had been considered for the past few years. Google eventually sorted the mess and moved on, making Gmail one of its biggest successes after Search.

When Sundar Pichai joined Google in 2004, Eric Schmidt was the CEO. Page and Brin had got the immensely capable former CEO and Chairman of Novell to join Google in 2001 when Page decided to step down.

Joining Google as one of the scores of Product Managers, Pichai's initial responsibilities related to Search and consumer products like the Google Toolbar, iGoogle and Desktop Search. For someone with Pichai's ambition and fervour to make changes, this may not have looked like an ideal beginning, at least not on the surface. After all, he was one among several product managers, barely touching the echelon of middle management at Google. And the products he had been given to handle were certainly not the kind of stuff you write home about or boast of at alumni meetings.

However, Pichai has been known to weather constraints and convert what others may see as a disadvantage into an opportunity. And he did just that with the otherwise innocuous-looking Google Toolbar.

'Tooling' it to the top

'Don't wait for extraordinary opportunities.
Seize common occasions and make them great.
Weak men wait for opportunities; strong men
make them.'

– Orison Swett Marden

Pichai's reasons for joining Google were perhaps no different from that of several other high-potential resources who had joined this amazing organization. What drove him to the legendary company was possibly the desire to change the world through technology that empowers people to do amazing things.

However, before he could begin to do that, he would need to accomplish something entirely different; something that might not have been as important or elevating as changing the world but was certainly critical for Google's survival. And it all started with the Google Toolbar!

The Toolbar was significant as it enabled Google to make its search engine the default option on Internet Explorer and Firefox, the two most popular browsers at the time. Pichai's role in creating Google's Chrome browser, and driving its success even while Microsoft demonstrated their aggression against it, was one of the things that propelled him to the limelight. Eric Schmidt was initially not in favour of a browser. The CEO of Google didn't see any point in replicating a product that was already doing well in the market. However, Pichai saw it differently. He argued that Microsoft might someday replace Google as the default search engine on Internet Explorer with one of their own. The face-off continued for a bit with neither party yielding. Pichai, in what is now known to be his patent style, waited and watched for the right opportunity to convince Schmidt and the others.

At long last, the Chrome project was approved by Schmidt in April 2006. It was none too soon, either. Six months later, the team at Google had their most fiendish ghosts come alive. Microsoft had just shaken up their world as they knew it, and the Bill Gates-led company had done it without providing any notice to either Google or to the users. The date was 18 October 2006. Microsoft had, without warning, changed the default search engine on Internet Explorer to Bing.

In order to understand the importance of this move, it will be significant to consider how Google was making its money at that time. Internet Explorer was moving traffic of millions of customers to Google since the latter had been the default engine on Microsoft's browser. This traffic was worth billions of dollars to Google. While Google was also the default search engine on every other browser of note (including Firefox), close to 65 per cent of its users came through Internet Explorer.

Microsoft's move to make Bing the default search engine on Internet Explorer resulted in Google losing close to 300 million customers! This wasn't just a business setback. It was the kind of nightmare you might wake up from to find out that you are no longer in business.

Fortunately for Google, Sundar Pichai had foreseen this. Along with his team, Pichai went into crisis mode. The net result was a dual strategy. Google made use of a feature in Internet Explorer and created a pop-up window rooted in the web page. This gave customers, who were now on Bing, the option of setting their default back to Google. This was helpful and somewhat saved the day for the Search leader. Nearly 60 per cent of the lost customers reverted to using Google.

However, this was not yet enough to allow Google to breathe easy. There were still approximately a 100 million customers to win back. This is where the innocuous Google Toolbar came into the picture. The Toolbar affords a search box that always points to Google. This meant that any customer with the Google Toolbar installed would be recaptured and reverted to Google. Also, the latter could check the registry settings, thereby prompting users to change the default, if need be.

While Pichai and his team at Google had won the battle, they knew that the war was just beginning. Microsoft was not an easy competitor and the software firm was entirely capable of coming up with measures in the future that would prevent Google from recovering its lost customers. The next time could be fatal for Google. Pichai and the powers-that-be at Google were in no mood to wait for such a moment to happen in the future.

Pichai swung into action and began signing up OEM bundling deals. Distributors, including the likes of Hewlett Packard (HP) and other large players were spoken to and the result was that Google's software bundle was pre-installed on millions of computers. This ensured that when a customer bought a computer, it would have Google Toolbar, Google Desktop and other software already installed on it. Google would either be set as a default search engine or the user would be prompted to change the existing search engine back to Google the first time they used the browser. Sundar Pichai and team had saved Google from a major potential disaster.

This event did two things. On the personal front, it positioned Pichai as a forward-looking visionary resource, a perception that at once differentiated him from the several other sharp-shooting cerebral product managers at Google. On the other hand, it set the ball rolling in the right direction for the creation of Google's own browser, a product that would later be called Chrome and shake up the world of Internet Explorer and Microsoft.

Chrome shines

'He likes scale, huge scale. I was in the room when Sundar convinced Eric Schmidt that it would be possible to unseat Internet Explorer as the world's most popular browser.'

– Christopher Sacca

It's fair to say that Pichai's current success owes a great deal to his ability to lead difficult projects successfully; among these, in the initial stages, were the Toolbar and Chrome. The former was significant in defending Google's search efforts on users' machines whereas the latter took that one step forward by improving the user's experience of the entire web. At the outset, Sundar Pichai had figured out the key to Google's ongoing success: keep users online and they would keep using Google for Search.

Pichai's vision of having a Google browser came at an interesting time. Google and Microsoft had been battling it out on various fronts ever since Google became a noticeable player on the horizon. The charismatic leader of Microsoft, Bill Gates, has been quoted innumerable times saying that he would drive Google to the ground in the war for innovation and customers. Microsoft has rarely been able to make this reality. Google with its nimble structure and an almost maniacal obsession with innovation more often than not has frustrated Microsoft's efforts. This has not gone down too well with the gigantic software company that in the early 2000s still considered Google to be an upstart that could be put in its place.

It did not help that the Google founders and CEO Eric Schmidt failed to show any public deference to the Redmond-based company. If anything, they faced Microsoft head-on the first opportunity they got. In 2005, Eric Schmidt spoke at the University of Washington's Paul Allen Center for Computer Science and Engineering, a venue donated and named after one of the Microsoft founders. Schmidt was at his best. He was respectful enough not to come across as brash in his views about Microsoft but outspoken enough to get his goal across: he wanted to lure into Google's work force as many talented people as he could. And talent taken away from the University of Washington was talent made unavailable to the nearby headquarters of Microsoft. It was like putting your arm inside the lion's den and attempting to take away its food while it slumbered nearby! Schmidt referred to Google as the best place in the world to work while his comments about Microsoft plainly indicated that the latter was a sleeping monolith whose best days were behind it.

Again, the same year, Google hired a man called Dr Kai-Fu Lee in China. Lee had been Microsoft's key man in China since 1998 and his relationships within China were incomparable. While several senior managers from Microsoft had already joined Google, Lee's decision to join Google was seen as one of the highest-ranking exits from Microsoft. This did not go down well with Steve Ballmer, CEO of Microsoft, and the battle-lines were drawn much tighter between Google and the older organization.

Later, in 2005, Google dealt another large blow to Microsoft. Google already had a tie-up with America Online (AOL). However, in December 2005, it was able to frustrate bids from rival companies Yahoo and Microsoft, resulting in a $1 billion deal with AOL that saw Google take up a 5 per cent stake in the company. The strategic partnership with AOL meant that Google could now further its search and advertising relationship with it. It was a big blow for Microsoft.

Perhaps, the biggest thorn in Microsoft's side involved its failed bid to acquire Yahoo. In 2008,

Microsoft's Ballmer launched a hostile bid to take over Yahoo. The offer price of $31 for Yahoo shares was significantly higher than the then stock price of $19. The $45 billion bid would not only have essentially placed Microsoft as a major contender in the Search business, but the overall combined entity would have been an invincible foe for Google or any other player in the industry. However, the Google troika (Larry Page, Sergey Brin and Eric Schmidt) successfully rallied Jerry Yang (the Yahoo chief). The result was an advertisement pact between the two companies that enabled Google to help Yahoo make more advertisement money through Google's superior technology. Yahoo was able to successfully ward off the hostile bid. Microsoft knew they would have to do something about Google before it became too big to handle.

All of this might still not have been sufficient cause for Microsoft to really target Google's lifeline – its ad business. That owed its basis to something else, an event that happened in 2004.

It started with Google going public in August 2004. Until the company was privately held, its incredible profitability was known only to the Google founders, CEO Eric Schmidt, and a few other trusted people within the company. When it went public, the company had to disclose its immense revenue and profitability data. What had seemed like a modest-sized Search firm till then to the public, and even to its competitors, now suddenly loomed as a gigantic Search organization earning billions of dollars in revenue every year. That most of the money came from ads was not lost on anyone and no one was more acutely aware of Google's cash inflows than Microsoft. The reasoning at Redmond did not need a genius to decipher – cut off the ad revenue to Google and the company would die. And if the same business could be replicated at Microsoft, it would be like killing two birds with one stone. Pichai and others at Google did not fail to see this either. The blatant replacement of Google with Bing on Internet Explorer had put the writing clearly on the wall and it helped Pichai get the green light from Schmidt and others to commence building a browser from the Google stable.

Pichai knew that Microsoft had, to a large extent, been responsible for driving Netscape out of business. Netscape had, in 1995, gone public with a stock price of $28. The stock price went up by almost 300 per cent within a day of it being traded. When Microsoft came out with Internet Explorer in August 1995, Netscape had more than 80 per cent of the browser market share. Microsoft responded by signing exclusive contracts with ISPs and bundling Internet Explorer with its Windows OS. In 1998, AOL announced a $4.2 billion acquisition for Netscape. By the time the deal fructified in 1999, it was worth almost $10 billion.

Pichai knew what Microsoft was capable of. He did not want a similar fate for Google. The first thing was to avoid reliance on Internet Explorer as that allowed Microsoft to replace Google Search as the default on their browser. This underscored the need for Google's own browser. Hence, Chrome was born. The next, equally important thing, was to ensure that Microsoft could not do to Chrome what it had done to Netscape. One of the issues with Netscape was that it was not free for users, especially corporations, whereas Internet Explorer (IE 2.0) from Microsoft was free for all Windows users, even if they were commercial businesses. Google Chrome was consequently offered free to all users.

Chrome was a big hit with users with its few significant advantages over Microsoft's browser. Chrome had more effective memory management. The page navigation was intelligent compared not just to the Internet Explorer but also to other popular browsers of the time. The text layout and rendering was faster, too.

According to StatCounter, in January 2009 Chrome had a market share of 1.38 per cent compared to

Internet Explorer's significantly larger 65.41 per cent. Exactly one year later, Chrome had notched it up to 6.04 per cent whereas Internet Explorer's share fell to 55.25 per cent. The real difference, however, came in July 2011 when Chrome considerably reduced the gap between Internet Explorer and itself. At this stage, Chrome was at 22.14 per cent while Internet Explorer was at approximately twice its share at 42.45 per cent. A year later, by July 2012, Chrome (33.81 per cent) comfortably beat Internet Explorer (32.04 per cent).

By February 2015, Chrome was seated atop a comfortable 48.71 per cent while Explorer languished at an unimpressive 18.91 per cent, according to the StatCounter Global desktop stats figures.

Today, Pichai says, one-third of the world's users are on Google Chrome. In the consumer space, the share could actually be higher, given that Google has historically been stronger on the consumer end compared to Microsoft's relative strengths on the enterprise side. Also, enterprise users take a while to upgrade and that could be another reason they are still on Internet Explorer. It's noteworthy that emerging markets have shown a higher preference for the faster Chrome. What is most interesting, though, is that there are more Windows users on Chrome than there are Mac users. This is possibly because Chrome initially launched on Windows.

Pichai's push on Chrome came at a time when even senior Googlers like Eric Schmidt felt that the world did not need an extra browser. One wonders if Chrome would have ever been born if the equation between Microsoft and Google hadn't been what it was in the early 2000s and if Google hadn't perceived a threat from the larger organization. Be that as it may, Chrome is currently the predominant player in the browser market. Not only that, Chrome (the browser) is the basis for Chrome OS (the Google operating system); Google looks set to push Chrome OS as an alternative to Microsoft Windows.

Chrome – not just a browser

> *'Sundar has a talent for creating products that are technically excellent yet easy to use; and he loves a big bet.'*
>
> – Larry Page

Following the immense success of Google Chrome, Sundar Pichai was promoted to the post of vice president. This was followed by another promotion to senior vice president a short while later.

In 2008, Pichai successfully steered Google to the browser game with the launch of Chrome. A year later, he was at it again; this time the focus was the web-based Chrome OS for netbooks and desktop machines. Most people familiar with Pichai's thinking surmise that the Chrome OS was perhaps the long-term plan behind Google's browser – the idea that the Chrome OS would eventually provide a viable alternative to Microsoft Windows.

Google is willing and ready to take the battle where it matters, not just to Microsoft Windows but Apple iOS, too. After all, Google has reiterated many a times that it wants to be to smart phones what Microsoft is to desktops, that it wants to rule the roost in the smart phone market through Android. Therefore, while on the one hand Pichai is trying to integrate Chrome and Android to give a unified experience to smart phone users, on the other hand Google's game plan is to ignite the smart phone war between the Google-backed Android system and Apple's iOS.

From Google's perspective, Chrome would veritably be the browser by choice in all Android-powered smart phones. This would be feasible when users of these devices cease to see Chrome and Android as separate from each other. This has been one of Pichai's key deliverables.

Chrome OS was launched in July 2009. Pichai and Google explained it as an operating system where both applications as well as data would reside in Cloud, and which automatically updates to the latest version.

Later in 2009, as of the Chromium OS project, Google made the source code for Chrome OS available to developers who could modify the code and build their own versions. The Chrome OS, though, is supported solely by Google and its partners and runs on hardware that has been designed towards this objective. Among its various differentiated features the one that stands out is the incredible speed at which the operating system boots up. At a conference in 2009, Sundar Pichai demonstrated how the Chrome OS could boot up in a mere seven seconds!

Hardware featuring Chrome OS started retailing in May 2011. The Chromebook, which is a laptop with Chrome OS as its operating system, was announced at the Google I/O conference in May 2011, and was available for shipping the following month. While the initial Chromebooks were in partnership with Acer and Samsung, by 2013 Lenovo and HP also entered the fray. Soon thereafter, Google itself joined in. Samsung introduced a desktop version of the Chromebook in mid-2012. This was called the Chromebox. A year-and-a-half later, in January 2014, LG Electronics came up with an all-in-one device called Chromebase. The latter had Chromebox hardware inside a monitor accompanied with a built-in camera, microphone and speakers. Some time later, a slightly different version of the Chromebase was introduced by Acer. This one came with a touch screen. Earlier this year, Google launched the Chromebit. The Chromebit is a dongle running the Chrome OS. When it is inserted into the HDMI slot of a television set or a computer monitor, the Chromebit turns the display screen into a personal computer.

A comparison of the Chrome OS with Microsoft Windows shows why the Chrome OS just might be Microsoft's biggest nightmare after the Chrome browser. The cost of the operating system is of course an area of concern. While Windows OS comes free when a user buys a Windows laptop, subsequent updates do cost a fair share of money. In comparison, the Chrome OS updates do not cost the user a penny. The cherry on the cake is that it updates in a fraction of the time that Windows updates need.

Another advantage of the Chrome OS is that Chromebooks come with SSD (solid state drive) as compared to HDD (hard disk drive) format on Windows laptops. While there are various advantages to SSDs, the pertinent fact is that it allows Chrome OS products like the Chromebook to boot up with incomparable speed. In fact, the fastest Windows laptop would possibly be slower than the slowest Chromebook. Likewise, the performance of a Chromebook would change ever so slightly with time whereas a Windows laptop would generally degrade over time, given the significant overhead of the Windows OS and the slow-spinning HDD on it.

More importantly, aspects like increased battery time and security issues are significant for today's users. Chromebooks with the Chrome OS have considerably longer battery life and are practically immune to malware and viruses.

The successful launch of the Chrome browser made Pichai a known entity within Google. The introduction of Chrome OS and subsequent related products now established him as someone to be reckoned with within the rapidly growing company.

People skills really matter

'The best executive is the one who has sense enough to pick good men to do what he wants done, and self-restraint to keep from meddling with them while they do it.'

– Theodore Roosevelt

Pichai started at Google with the rather unsexy Google Toolbar and we saw what he did with that. The launch of Google Chrome and the Chrome OS were two more feathers in his cap and they certainly got him a lot of attention at Google's headquarters. Over the years, Sundar Pichai was given charge of

Google Apps. This was previously headed by Dave Girouard, vice president for Google Apps who had been responsible for Gmail, Google Calendar, Google Docs, and other cloud applications. One of the reasons cited behind Larry Page's decision to get Sundar to take over from Dave was for Pichai to lessen the gap between consumer and enterprise apps. A year later, Pichai got what was perhaps his biggest break, when he replaced Andy Rubin as the head of Android in 2013. (For the uninitiated, Andy Rubin was co-founder and CEO of Android before Google acquired the company in 2005 for approximately $50 million.) Later in 2014, Page made Pichai the overall head of Products for Google, with the exception of entities like YouTube, Google X, Calico and a few other divisions.

Pichai had an unprecedented rise within Google, a company that has scores of bright, young, competitive people working for it and it is interesting to take a look into how he did this. Much as Nadella did at Microsoft a year ago, Pichai's key strength lies in his ability to manage people and get them to collaborate with each other in a manner that borders on leadership mastery. At his core, Pichai is an empathic individual. When he says he cares for people, he really means it. This has been borne out by several colleagues who cite the example of Pichai sitting for hours outside his former boss's (Marissa Mayer) office so he could present a particular case for his team members in a positive light. That degree of fidelity towards team members not only earns tremendous loyalty from people, it also sets up perceptions of the manager's attitude towards the entire team.

While no one would call Pichai aggressive or arrogant, there are few who would dare to call him non-assertive. If anything, Pichai is a classic example of assertive behaviour. While he doesn't go out of his way to court conflict, he has been at his sterling best when managing conflict, irrespective of the magnitude or context.

This was evident when Eric Schmidt disagreed with his proposal of a browser to compete with Internet Explorer. Pichai did not back down; neither did he get into confrontation mode. He waited for the right moment, and when it came he was ready to dive into the enormous amount of work that was required to launch Google Chrome.

Likewise, his diplomacy and people skills were evident when it came to dealing with Samsung in 2014. Google felt that Samsung might have been giving less importance to selling Google services like its apps store, Google Play, because of vested interests of the South Korean company. As the man who led Android, Pichai was tasked with addressing the situation. It was a challenging task. Samsung was a key partner for Google, yet it had to be sent a clear message, and in a manner that did not upset the ties between the two companies. Pichai met with Shin, Samsung's CEO. He focused on the two companies' mutual goals and the synergies thereof. The meeting was successful. Samsung agreed to scale back Magazine UX, a customizable user interface designed by Samsung and one of the major reasons for Google's dissonance. This ensured that Samsung devices would stay closer to Android. At Google's end, the decision to sell Motorola to Lenovo (at a significantly lower price of $2.9 billion than the $12.5 billion they had acquired it for) was seen by a lot of people as a gesture to pacify Samsung. Most third-party Android manufacturers, including Samsung, believed Motorola had access to Android innovations before they had. Be that as it may, the Google-Samsung fracas ended and with it Pichai's reputation as an able negotiator as well as a people's man received a further boost.

One of the biggest challenges that Pichai has faced at Google was taking over Android. When Larry Page declared that Sundar Pichai would take over Android from Andy Rubin, there was a large measure of scepticism and debate. After all, Andy Rubin was not just the man who had created Android and sold it to Google, he had successfully built a team at Google that was able to install the Android OS on hundreds of millions of smart phones all over the world. Why then was Rubin replaced with Pichai? This question was the talk of the town until one actually looked under the surface to understand Larry Page's reasoning.

One of the reasons, of course, could be the difference in how Andy and Page viewed Android. Andy Rubin viewed Samsung – one of Google's key partners – as potential threat to Android. Rubin's logic was that the South Korean company could at some time in the future re-write Android's code in sync with Samsung's interests, and that eventually Samsung may even stop referring to Android. Therefore, it wasn't surprising that Andy viewed Motorola (which Google had acquired earlier) as a protection against such an eventuality. The discomfort to Samsung (as well as other third-party manufacturers of Android-led devices) apart, this view of Android was considered too narrow by Larry Page and he felt it confined Google's future interests. Page – like Pichai – had a contrarian view. In his opinion, Android was not the final goal for Google, but more of a means to achieve that goal. Page saw Google more as a cloud services organization; a business that was structured around products like Search, Gmail, YouTube and Google

Maps, among others. Android fitted into Page's philosophy insofar as it enabled Google to develop partnerships with hardware manufacturers like Samsung to make the other core services of Google available to users. In Page's view, therefore, Samsung (and others like the South Korean company) were not a potential threat, but a major potential ally in the war against Microsoft and Apple.

What Android had definitely achieved under Rubin was that it had broken Apple's dominance in the smart phones market. This was good, but the future of Google was more aligned to Pichai's way of thinking. Added to this was the fact that Pichai had already earned his stripes forging strong partnerships with PC manufacturers for the Google Toolbar when he wanted Toolbar pre-loaded on machines to counter the threat from Microsoft. Those partnerships and what they yielded for Google were critical in keeping users connected to Google Search. Given that background, Larry Page evidently wanted Pichai to repeat the same process with hardware manufacturers by getting them to install software access points to Google's core services. It was immaterial to Page whether those software access points were Android, or anything else for that matter.

The other thing was that while Pichai was the man behind Chrome and Rubin the one behind

Android, the powers-that-be at Google envisaged the two different operating systems converging towards becoming a unified software platform, making it easier for users. Pichai echoed this view, citing his belief that Android and Chrome were executions of two different philosophies on personal computing. His goal was to ensure that the applications even looked the same across platforms since users would be immune to the underlying technology as long as the interface was seamless. Pichai's job to align the two operating systems – Android and Chrome – was clear. Now, he would need to put all the grit he could muster into making it happen.

The other challenge of course was more behavioural. It had to do with the rather different management styles of Rubin and Pichai. Under Rubin, Android was being run as a separate company within Google and, whether consciously or inadvertently, silos had popped up while Rubin was in charge of the division. The work environment was more than tense between Android and other parts of Google. Even within his team there was a fair measure of conflict. Pichai, on the other hand, was known to be a calm and collected person. Page decided that Pichai fitted the bill perfectly. He wasn't wrong. Within a couple of months of taking over Android, Pichai worked his magic and the trouble within Android as well as the strain with other businesses evaporated. It was as if there had never been any problem.

Pichai had yet again proven that he was not merely a man of numbers and a brilliant engineer. He has a rare knack for not just collecting valuable insights but blending them with softer issues that make people want to extend themselves without being asked to do so.

The Midas touch

'There's no question, the guy who runs it has the Midas touch.'

– Bill Bishop

In the eleven years that Pichai has been at Google, he has demonstrated an uncanny ability to focus on products and solutions that have worked wonders for the Mountain View based company.

While a few people might be tempted to attribute his success to luck and fortune favouring the Chennai bred man, it would be an incredible fate that would ensure success for every product gambit from Pichai in the past decade or more.

Sundar's success in actuality owes a great deal to his ability to listen to people and derive cues from what is happening around him. It is that extraordinary ability to seek an outside – in perspective that allows him to overlay his own analysis and gumption to come up with a winning formula every time. Google's secret sauce in the early days might have been their algorithm and the immense computing power their networked computers wrought for them. Pichai's success lies in paying attention to what is happening around him and blending it with an uncanny sense for what will work.

The success with the Google Toolbar at the time of joining Google is a classic case in point. Where others might have viewed it as an unglamorous product, Pichai saw in it tremendous opportunity to mitigate a potential threat from Microsoft. However, mere success with the Toolbar would certainly not have placed him where he is today.

Sundar Pichai saw what a lot of other people, including legendary leaders like Eric Schmidt, missed seeing initially. The first such insight was the inherent danger of Google not having its own browser, especially when it was the single largest Search company in the world. The fact that the most widely used browser at the time came from a company (Microsoft) that was not necessarily invested in Google's success made it even more ominous. It wouldn't have taken Microsoft too much to cut off Google's air supply and it is fortunate for Google that eventuality did not come to bear early in their life-cycle. By the time it happened, Pichai and his team were well on their way to launching Google Chrome. Chrome quickly snatched market share from Internet Explorer and the other popular browsers. At the time of writing this, Google owns one-third of the market share of browsers globally.

Pichai has gone on record to say, 'Chrome grew roughly 300 per cent last year. We have hundreds of millions of active users. We have many ways of looking at it. You can argue about the data, but in general I think we have gained substantial mindshare since we've launched the product. I think it's fair to say that we are number one or number two in all countries in the world. It's fair to say that roughly a third of people are using Chrome; I think it's much more than a third in the consumer space.'[6]

The success of Google Chrome was followed soon after by the Chrome OS and the related products it helped spawn at Google. Chrome OS has rapidly transformed the way people look at personal computing, and its ramifications on the future of the industry will be far-reaching. The Chromebook has literally taken the education world by storm. It represents one-third of the laptops purchased by education institutions, especially in the US. This is almost at par with Apple MacBooks (32 per cent) and just below Microsoft's share of 39 per cent despite the fact that the latter two have been around much longer than Chromebooks. Not just Chromebooks, the Chrome OS has helped power products like Chromebit, Chromecast and Chromebox among others. Chrome OS also becomes a tool in the hands of Google to get products like Gmail and Google Docs into the hands of as many users as possible. In the end, it is not just about selling products to customers – something that Google is doing fairly well anyway – but more to do with making computing more accessible to people, irrespective of whether they are in the US or in an emerging market.

Let's look at the position Pichai was in when he replaced Andy Rubin. Taking over from Andy Rubin was a challenging task in itself. Rubin had not just developed a great product; he had enabled hundreds of millions of Android-powered smart phones in the hands of users. It was a tough act for anyone to follow. Pichai made it look easy. In 2014 more than one billion Android smart phones were sold globally. This represented 80.7 per cent of the global market share of smart phones. Apple iOS sales accounted for 15.4 per cent while Windows phones languished at 2.8 per cent. Blackberry contributed 0.6 per cent. One of the things that Pichai worked on was to get emerging markets hooked on to the Internet. This heralded the launch of Android One, which has as its objective making low-cost, good-quality phones available to users in emerging markets. India and Philippines are among the countries where Android One has already been launched.

Having a pulse on what the customer wants is one of Pichai's core strengths. Let's hope that continues to hold him in good stead as he takes on the might of stalwarts like Apple, Microsoft, Amazon and others in the dynamic world of technology.

This bird's feathers rarely get ruffled

'There are plenty of difficult obstacles in your path. Don't allow yourself to become one of them.'

– Ralph Marston

While much has been said about Pichai's people skills and his business acumen, one of the things that sets him apart as a leader par excellence is his ability to stay calm and collected even in the face of extreme pressure. Not just that, he is also able to get others to relax and focus on what needs to be done. More than anything else, that is the hallmark of a true leader and Pichai appears to have demonstrated this leadership trait even when he wasn't counted among the senior leadership at Google.

When Chrome was launched, Pichai took on the rather onerous task of talking to Apple and Mozilla to ensure the relationship with them was not impacted. After all, Apple is the maker of Safari and Mozilla owns Firefox. Chrome would end up being a competitor for both Safari and Mozilla. Pichai was able to balance the objective of coming up with their own browser without making Apple or Mozilla feel threatened in any way. As a result of the calm and diplomatic handling of the situation, the relationships remained strong.

Another instance of Pichai's calm attitude was visible during the launch of Chrome. Google had planned an innovative promotion and communication strategy for the yet-to-be-launched browser. A 38-page comic book had been prepared by the marketing team. Among other things, the comic book explained the unique attributes of Chrome. Since the launch of Chrome was happening around May Day, the comic book was posted to media persons and bloggers in such a way that it would reach their mailboxes at the end of the long weekend. Unfortunately for Google, the comic books reached Germany earlier than intended as there was no holiday there. A German blogger promptly put the comic book online. Understandably, there was rampant confusion and everyone from Marissa Mayer (Pichai's boss at that time) down to Pichai and other team members were summoned to Google's headquarters.

The situation could have gone either way. It could either have been the biggest marketing blunder of the decade or be effectively contained. This is where Pichai yet again exhibited his uncanny control and composure. When he addressed a room full of more than 100 people, he made everyone feel that he was aware of them. There was no anger seeping through him. Nor was there any instance where he placed blame on anyone. Pichai's attitude was entirely matter-of-fact and focused on how everyone present could resolve the crisis effectively. It enabled others to centre in on what they could do rather than bemoan what had already happened. As it transpired, the launch of Chrome (despite the slip-up) went off successfully and made for a perfect coming-out party for Sundar Pichai. The man whom very few people outside, and not too many within Google at the time knew had taken the first gigantic step on the path that would eventually lead him to the most coveted role at Google.

Twitter's loss, Google's gain!

'Life has no limitations, except the ones you make.'

– Les Brown

In December 2010, Dick Costolo took over as CEO of Twitter after former CEO and co-founder Ev Williams stepped down to play a more active role in product development. This shifted the equation for Jason Goldman who until then was head and vice-president of product at Twitter. Since Goldman did not at once join any of the usual suspects – Google, Facebook and Instagram, among others – it was widely surmised that he may have left fearing a lessening of his influence within the product role at Twitter.

Twitter made an aggressive bid to woo Sundar Pichai at this juncture. Satya Patel was the other choice, though analysts suggest that Patel was an alternative if – and only if – Pichai didn't join Twitter. Patel had previously been a product manager at DoubleClick and later at Google after the latter acquired the company.

At this stage, Google had already been facing employee exits, something the Search giant hadn't been used to in their early years. A majority of the people exiting Google were leaving to join the new rockstar on the block – Facebook – and several other hot startups. Truth be told, what was happening at Google was a reflection of what had happened a few years ago at Microsoft, with talented professionals leaving the Redmond-based giant for newer, more active pastures. Facebook was now the new Google, and Google was trying hard not to become the old Microsoft.

While the Facebook staff strength was barely 10 per cent of Google at the time that Twitter decided to make an offer to Pichai, the fact was that close to 200 Googlers had already left for the social media company. It wouldn't have mattered so much to Google; after all, that number represented barely 1 per cent of the total Google force at the time. The issue was that lately some of the senior folks at Google had also moved out. This included the likes of Sheryl Kara Sandberg and Erick Tseng. Sandberg, a Harvard graduate, was formerly vice-president for global online sales and operations at Google. In 2008, however, Mark Zuckerberg decided she was perfect for the role of COO at Facebook. Sandberg was weaned away from Google in March 2008 and was largely responsible for making Facebook a profitable business. Erick Tseng, who had earlier worked with Microsoft and Yahoo, had been a senior product manager at Google, working on Android. The former

MIT–Stanford graduate also left Google in 2010 to take over as head of mobile products at Facebook.

Needless to say, the spate of exits of highly talented resources was a source of deep concern for Google. In a few cases, Google had offered significant financial benefits even to relatively junior level engineers in order to keep them from moving to Facebook and Twitter. Twitter's imminent offer to one of their key resources (Pichai) had them in a twirl. It would have been a severe blow for Google, not just because Pichai was by then a fairly senior resource at Google, but more so because his moving out would have left the recently launched Chrome and Chrome OS rudderless.

In retrospect, it is possible that there was a third consideration for trying to keep Pichai at Google. While this might not have been evident in 2010, subsequent events do indicate that Larry Page might perhaps have begun to view Pichai as a high-potential resource for the company; someone who could possibly be groomed to take on much higher responsibilities within Google. The $50 million cash plus stock award to Pichai to keep him at Google was in that light, a minor way for the company to demonstrate their commitment to Pichai's continued success and elevation within Google. As soon as Larry Page took over as CEO from Eric Schmidt in 2011, among his first actions was making Sundar Pichai senior vice-president of product at Google. And since then, without exception, Pichai has continued to add feathers in his cap in terms of responsibility and additional roles. What began in 2010 culminated in 2015 with Larry Page bringing Pichai to the helm of Google. To say that all of this was merely to hold Pichai back from joining either Twitter or Facebook would be silly. While it may certainly have played a role in the earlier days when Twitter offered to hire Pichai, in subsequent years Pichai has reached milestones every step of his way to get where he is today.

The other man on the block

In the last two years, two men have made India very proud. While there are differences between the two – some subtle and others distinct – there are quite a few similarities too.

In February 2014, a man from Hyderabad was named CEO of the legendary Microsoft. Nadella is a down-to-earth man, a people's person with very strong home-grown values. Mostly educated in India in non-metros, he made it on his own merit in the US. While he did work with another company (Sun Microsystems) for a brief period before joining Microsoft, Nadella has been with the Redmondheadquartered company ever since. Satya Nadella is only the third CEO of Microsoft after Bill Gates and Steve Ballmer.

Sundar Pichai was born in a small town called Madurai and raised in Chennai. As with Nadella, Pichai's education was also centred in Chennai and later in Kharagpur. Pichai, also a people's person and an unassuming man, exhibits a significant value system. Like Nadella, he too made it on his own merit in the US. Though Pichai worked with two companies (Applied Materials and McKinsey) prior to joining Google, he has been with the Search giant ever since. Pichai is only the third CEO of the company after Eric Schmidt and Larry Page, even though Page served two terms (at different times) as CEO.

In the dog-eat-dog world of corporate politics, both Nadella and Pichai have managed to maintain their equilibrium and have mastered the art of getting things done without indulging in petty politics. In each case, people around them have said it would be difficult to find someone who has a problem with him in the organization. That in itself speaks for the incredible people skills of these two capable men.

Another similarity between the two is that both men have worked on the browser act of their individual companies. Nadella has worked wonders for Microsoft in some quarters with Bing. Pichai's contribution of course, is the kind of stuff legends are made of as far as Google Chrome is concerned.

Both men realize the importance of Cloud and mobile development for the future of the industry. While Nadella has pulled in third-party phone manufacturers like Karbonn, Micromax, Lava (Xolo), Lenovo, LG and Prestigio, among others, to launch low-cost, high-quality smart phones in emerging markets, Pichai's strategy hasn't been too different in the case of Android.

On cloud services, there is a bit of a difference between the two. Pichai has Google leveraging their cloud services through Chrome. Further, Google has Android, an open source OS mainly for mobile devices which is integrated with their cloud services. Chrome and Android are both free and Google's open-source culture compares vividly with the rather proprietary approach of Microsoft. Google leverages the integration between their browser and OS to channelize traffic to their online services, thereby enhancing their returns. Android, too, creates value by driving traffic to Google's services rather than focusing merely on the operating system.

Microsoft possibly needs to drop its immense focus on the operating system and start treading a different path. The positive thing for Microsoft is that unlike his predecessor (Steve Ballmer), Nadella sees the new world as being one of connected devices, big data and cloud services. This suggests that Nadella is aware that Microsoft's future is not restricted to Windows but needs to be one which is a mobile, Cloud and connected device world in which the operating system will become less and less relevant when compared to the cloud services that it connects to.

While Twitter's offer to Pichai in 2010 has been widely known and talked about, relatively few people are aware that Pichai was also being considered for the position of CEO at Microsoft in 2014. It is difficult to ascertain the veracity of this, but it certainly throws up some interesting thoughts, especially if one were to compare the two in retrospect for the Microsoft CEO role.

For one, Pichai has dealt with consumer-based businesses and has a pulse on the mind of the customer. Nadella's strengths on the enterprise side are irrefutable. He has headed Cloud and enterprise at Microsoft prior to his ascension as CEO and these have been the most profitable areas for the company. Pichai probably scores a point over Nadella inasmuch as he has experience in both the PC (Chrome) and the mobile (Android) spaces. Given that Microsoft has struggled on the mobile front, Pichai would have definitely brought value to Microsoft from that perspective. However, Nadella's strength in enterprise balances this, as enterprise has been and still is a major source of growth and revenue for Microsoft. Nadella's biggest asset, though, would have been his deep understanding and appreciation of the Microsoft culture which is very unlike that of Google. Where Pichai might have struggled (resistance from long-standing Microsoft staff), Nadella would stand to gain a more favourable acceptance in this area.

In an ideal world, a perfect solution for Microsoft would perhaps have been a combination of Satya Nadella and Sundar Pichai as CEO. That would indeed have been a game-changer for the company. It would have brought in the best from the consumer and the enterprise sides, and balanced strengths on mobile and Cloud as well. However, that is one story that probably won't get written now.

Both Nadella and Pichai have shown themselves eminently capable of adapting to new challenges and continuously learning and evolving. In the last year, Nadella has demonstrated a fair share of that adaptability and has made changes that will have high impact in years to come. Pichai has shown he is capable of doing this in several roles in the last decade.

Both Google and Microsoft appear to be in very capable hands. It is a happy coincidence that both men are lovers of cricket. Time will tell whether it is the Hyderabadi who scores more points or the man from Chennai who bowls him out. In the meantime, it is going to be a great game to watch.

PART 3

THE ECOSYSTEM CALLED GOOGLE

'I feel there's an existential angst among young people. I didn't have that. They see enormous mountains, where I only saw one little hill to climb.'

– Sergey Brin

From origin to infinity

'Originality has nothing to do with producing something new; it is about seeking the source, the primordial ground from which you draw and have always drawn your being. It comes about when one works from one's origins, it is the dance of the eternal return... and is as ancient as the Dreamtime.'

– Billy Marshall Stoneking

They say if you want to know more about a person or an entity, it usually helps to know where they come from. Or, in other words, what has made them what they are today!

This couldn't be truer than in Google's case. In order to understand the Google eco-system it is imperative to understand the origins of the company and its founders. Without that the story of how a 41-year-old migrant from India (Sundar Pichai) became the CEO of one of the most valued and respected organizations in the world boxes its context. It will help us to understand why Google, born in 1998, was able to sweep past the legendary Microsoft. (It is noteworthy that when the co-founders of Google were still studying at Stanford and the current CEO of Google had not even landed in the US to pursue higher education, Microsoft was already a giant in the field.) Going back to the origin of Google will also enable a better understanding of the current culture there and why the powers-that-be at Mountain View continue to hold such store by innovation.

In short, if we want to predict the future of Google and the role its new CEO Sundar Pichai will play in it, we would first need to delve into the past and seek out the origins of this great firm, and that of its founders.

Difference of opinion is good

'Most of all, differences of opinion are opportunities for learning.'

– Terry Tempest Williams

Sergey Brin and Larry Page met on the Stanford campus in 1995. Brin was a gifted mathematician who had completed his undergraduate programme at the age of 19 and enrolled for the doctoral programme at Stanford. Page too had joined Stanford's highly competitive PhD programme. The two were not only different in their outlook – Brin was an extrovert while Page took a while to open up – they also enjoyed getting into debates with each one taking a different viewpoint. Sometimes they would take a contrarian point of view just for the sake of it; it got the creative juices running and kept their minds alert.

This verbal duelling and love for debate was not restricted to their stint at Stanford. This attitude defines the way the two founders still do things. Discussions are encouraged. A point of view, even if different, is allowed to be aired. And only when an issue has been discussed threadbare do the two founders rest.

While at Stanford, when Brin and Page were working on separate projects that would eventually blossom into Google, their dorm mates would occasionally get frustrated with their continuous banter. Gradually, what had been visible to Page and Brin all along dawned on others, too. If you wanted to have an open culture, it was important to be able to argue things transparently and without malice. More importantly, ongoing debates, even if they were sometimes contrived for the sake of a contrarian discussion were good; they kept the grey cells active and creative.

Over time, this habit of open debates and discussions – on every product Google launches or decides to launch – has stood the company in good stead. It has had a remarkable impact on framing the culture of the organization. Not just that, it keeps the multitude of highly talented resources at Google continuously on their toes and thinking creatively.

It was this culture of encouraging different opinions that enabled the relatively junior Pichai to suggest that the organization ought to have its own browser, when the CEO (Eric Schmidt) wasn't exactly hot on the idea. It also speaks a lot for the company that while Schmidt may not have seen eye to eye with Pichai on the topic initially, he finally did green-light the project. And the Google ecosystem along with Pichai and his team's hard work made Chrome one of their most successful products.

A small step for Google; a giant leap for mankind

'My job as a leader is to make sure everybody in the company has great opportunities, and that they feel they're having a meaningful impact and are contributing to the good of society. As a world, we're doing a better job of that. My goal is for Google to lead, not follow.'

– Larry Page

In August 1995, a tech company called Netscape went public. Within a day of trading, its stock price had gone up almost three times. In today's terms, it would possibly have achieved the status of a multi-bagger on the first day of trading. People began to speculate that Netscape might one day overshadow the by-then already legendary company called Microsoft.

Stanford, where Brin and Page were studiously trying to work towards their PhD, was agog with excitement. The energy was palpable and wherever one turned their eye, bright young students were thinking up ideas for the next big thing. It was fortuitous that Stanford was one of those places that encouraged the mingling of education and venture. Companies like Sun Microsystems had been born within the Stanford campus and faculty and students both knew there would be many more where that came from.

Meanwhile, Brin and Page were working on separate projects. Given that they were inseparable, it was natural for the two to discuss their work with each other. Soon, the germ of an idea was born, the result of a problem that begged to be solved at the time. At the time it was an ordeal to search for information on the web. Even though there were popular search engines like WebCrawler, Inktomi, Lycos, Infoseek and others, a user would have to wade through miles of data in order to get the right information. Brin and Page decided to try and find a solution to this problem. Working with their colleagues, and with the help of a few faculty members, they developed a link rating system called Page Rank. This was applied to the web and the first version of Google was born, which they called BackRub as it was concerned with back links to web pages. Finally, the name Google was chosen as a reference to Googol, a term that was reflective of a large number – the numerical 1 followed by a hundred zeros. The name was apt as Page and Brin planned to make it easy for users to search large amounts of information on the web.

In a short while, Google's user base grew. This required enormous computing power, which in turn needed a lot of computers. It meant funding. Initially, the duo managed to forage through junkyards and scrap to get components they could use to assemble their own machines. After a while they realized that the rate at which their user base and data was growing, they would need something more than the computers they had networked together with scrap and Lego material. Interestingly, one of the Yahoo cofounders (another Stanford alumnus) David Filo unwittingly played a small role in encouraging Brin and Page to set up a company that would very soon become a big competitor, and thereafter a much-needed ally against Microsoft. He advised Brin and Page to take a sabbatical from their PhD programme if they wanted to make Google a reality. The two did just that. By mid-1998, one of the co-founders of Sun Microsystems (Andy Bechtolsheim) had given them their first funding cheque made out for $100,000.

$25 million to start a revolution

'Search is extremely challenging, and improvements in the technology are significant. One hundred million web searches are performed every day. Quickly finding the right information is critical for web users in many professions. Google revolutionizes search technology and delivers information in a way that focuses on the user.'

– John Doerr

Kleiner Perkins Caufield & Byers was one of the most respected venture capital firms in Silicon Valley at the time Brin and Page were working on growing Google. The other one was Sequoia Capital. The former was represented by a legendary investor called John Doerr while Sequoia had the formidable Michael Moritz looking out for potential companies that could become big bets for his fund. Sequoia had invested $2 million in Yahoo earlier and had made a killing on the IPO. That the Yahoo founders were also from the Stanford stable was a coincidence. Moritz was not a man who invested based on sentiment. He did, however, see an opportunity for Google to become a probable vendor for Yahoo. John Doerr, on the other hand, was one of the investors in AOL and he laid a big bet on the potential of the Internet. That Google was in this space was very interesting for the man from Kleiner Perkins.

Google however had a different problem from most other start-ups. They had two giants from the venture capital universe, both wanting to invest in their company. The issue was that neither of them was comfortable co-investing. It was all or nothing, as far as Doerr and Moritz were concerned. For Brin and Page, this meant they would either have two of the top dogs in Silicon Valley sharing space with them in the boardroom, or neither of them. From their perspective, they were not too hot on either of the two VCs having control in the company. The only way this could be avoided was if both Sequoia and Kleiner Perkins invested together. It would still leave Page and Brin in control of the company.

After a lot of back and forth and considerable palpitations on all sides, the decision was made to invest $25 million (shared between the two VC firms). The deal was signed in June 1999.

Google now had the ammunition to take on larger players in Search. More importantly, they had strategically looped in two of the best-regarded men in Silicon Valley. Their mentoring and the network of people they brought with them would be worth more than the money they had put in. But for the moment, the fresh infusion of funds would enable Google to start the revolution that would soon spread to different corners of the civilized world.

The Search landscape

'The first rule of any technology used in a business is that automation applied to an efficient operation will magnify the efficiency. The second is that automation applied to an inefficient operation will magnify the inefficiency.'

– Bill Gates

In 1990, the Search industry underwent a dramatic change from the previous year when Alan Emtage created what was perhaps the world's first search engine called Archie. In 1991, Mark McCahill from the University of Minnesota came up with Gopher which searched for plain text reference in files, much like Archie did before it.

It is, however, Matthew Gray who is is credited with the development of a search engine in 1993, in a format we are familiar with today. Called Wandex, it used first of its kind technology to crawl the web to search the catalogue of indexed pages on the Internet.

It is interesting that two different forms of Search gained significance in the early nineties. One of them represented the Web directories that were popular in the initial phase; the other was the quintessential search engine, which in the latter part of the nineties was a preferred mode for web search.

Along with Wandex, another search engine called Excite made its mark in 1993. Like most projects revolving around the Internet, this too owed its origin to Stanford. Excite was one of the first engines to use statistical analysis of the relationship between words to enhance search relevancy on the web. While the Excite project commenced in 1993, its commercial release happened only in 1995.

Excite is one of those search engines that was badly affected with Google's entry in 1998. Finally, in 2004, Ask Jeeves (another Search portal) acquired Excite.

In 1994, two Stanford graduates, David Filo and Jerry Yang, started a company called Yahoo. While Yahoo considered itself more as an email company, it did provide Search through its Yahoo directories. These were manually edited and categorized. While they were initially popular, they were unable to keep up with the frenetic pace at which the web was growing. By the end of the 1990s, the Yahoo directories had completely lost steam. In order to make up for this, Yahoo placed a great deal of reliance on other search engines to boost the results it provided to its users. One of these search engines was Inktomi. Much later this was replaced with Google.

The other search engine to hit the market in 1994 was WebCrawler. Created by Brian Pinkerton from the University of Washington, it was the first of its kind in that it provided full text search. It was also one of the first engines to operate entirely based on advertising revenue within a year of going live. Later, Google used a very similar model though the advertising might have been managed in a different manner. WebCrawler was acquired by AOL in 1995. In a confusing move in 1997, Excite bought

WebCrawler from AOL. The plot thickened as Excite went bankrupt in 2001 and was in turn acquired by InfoSpace.

Lycos was the other big addition in 1994 to the Search wars. Developed by Michael Mauldin, Lycos's model was to operate on advertising revenue. By 1999, it was the most frequented site. In the latter part of the nineties, Lycos indulged in several acquisitions of Internet brands, including Wired Digital, the owner of HotBot. In 1999, USA Networks and Lycos signed a deal where the former would have acquired a 61.5 per cent stake in the company for approximately $20 billion but the deal fell through owing to shareholder angst at the complicated way in which it was structured. By mid-2000 however, Terra Networks acquired Lycos in a stock swap valued at $12.5 billion. Lycos went through a tumultuous period during the dotcom crash in 2001 and Terra Networks sold it to Daum Communications Corp for a mere $95.4 million.

Infoseek was yet another big player in the Search space that came into its own in 1994. It was a pay for use service founded by Steve Kirsch. In 1995, it became the default search engine for Netscape and this gave it tremendous leverage. In 1998, Disney acquired Infoseek and the latter bought over Excite. The following year, one of the Infoseek engineers – a man called Li Yanhong – moved to China and founded the search engine called Baidu.

Meanwhile, in 1995, a group of research scientists at DEC started AltaVista, which in a year's time began to provide exclusive search results for Yahoo. Two years down the line, in 1998, DEC itself was acquired by Compaq. During this period, AltaVista was possibly the most advanced search tool. In 2003, Overture acquired AltaVista for a mere $140 million, a minuscule amount compared to what it was worth (approximately $2.3 billion) in 2000, before the Internet bubble burst. Yahoo acquired Overture later the same year and hence became the owner of AltaVista, too.

Inktomi was one of the late entrants in the Search space and made itself visible in 1996. Founded by Eric Brewer and Paul Gauthier, they named the company after a mythical Indian spider. Inktomi was more than just a search engine. Its intent was to develop scalable software applications. Within one year, Inktomi had attracted the big daddy in the software sector. Microsoft started using Inktomi's search engine in 1998. The same year, Yahoo also made a decision to use Inktomi's search engine technology as their favoured choice. Inktomi's share price from the time of their IPO in June 1998 climbed from $18 to $130 within just five months. In 1999, AOL also began to use Inktomi's database to power its search engine, moving away from Excite. MSN, too, voted in favour of Inktomi, bidding adieu to AltaVista in the process. However, like its other contemporaries, Inktomi too lost tremendous steam in the aftermath of the dotcom bubble. It was finally acquired by Yahoo in 2003 for $235 million. As per the agreement, however, Inktomi continued to provide search results to MSN Search, a rival of Yahoo. At the same time, Google was providing the same service to Yahoo.

Ask Jeeves was born in 1996 and made public a year later. It was one of those companies that also acquired Excite. While it developed very strong brand loyalty among its users, its technology was unable to keep pace with the promises it made to prospective users and this seriously impacted its ability to make money. Eventually, they partnered with Google and, using Google's eco-system (popularly referred to as the Google Economy), Ask Jeeves made a significant turnaround.

Google came into the picture in 1998. Its PageRank link analysis algorithm was a runaway success and it began to make its mark in the Search landscape right from day one. It soon became the preferred choice as far as providing search results to companies like Yahoo, AOL and Netscape was concerned.

In 1998, Microsoft launched MSN Search (later called Windows Live). Until this time, Microsoft had focused on other areas as consumer Search was not really something they wanted to bet on. Plus they saw Email (and not Search) as the route to creating customers from an advertising standpoint. MSN Search initially displayed search results from Inktomi but by 2004 they started using their own built-in search results. Much later, this service was called Bing which would try and compete in a big way with Google Search.

Overture was almost a pioneer as far as paid search was concerned. Launched by Bill Gross in 1998, it made several high-powered acquisitions and was working with heavyweights like AOL and Yahoo among others. However, Google posed a big threat to them. The company led by Page and Brin was responsible for AOL dropping Overture in favour of Google.

As is evident here, during the nineties and the early part of the first decade in 2000, the Search landscape was peppered with several Search engineers, some of them accounting for the lion's share of the Search pie. However, Google was not just another Search engine. They had the best technology and over time they had ensured they hired top talent.

Talent matters

'When you're in a startup, the first ten people will determine whether the company succeeds or not. Each is 10 per cent of the company. So why wouldn't you take as much time as necessary to find all the A players? If three were not so great, why would you want a company where 30 per cent of your people are not so great? A small company depends on great people much more than a big company does.'

– Steve Jobs

One of the things that has differentiated Google from its competitors has been the top-notch talent they have striven to hire. Even back when they were a startup they ensured that every resource was handpicked.

Interestingly, the Google founders have been particular about hiring only engineers. What that means is that you could be an MBA from Wharton or Harvard but if you didn't have an engineering degree to go along with it you wouldn't clear too many levels during the hiring process at Google. Or you could be an economist par excellence, yet you would still need to have a background in technology if you really wanted to impress the founding duo.

In fact Eric Schmidt (the first CEO of Google) was

not hired because of his impressive track record in business (Eric was formerly CEO of Novell and had also worked at Sun Microsystems and Bell Labs). What attracted Page and Brin to Schmidt was his impeccable engineering background. Schmidt was a graduate in electrical engineering from Princeton. Later he picked up a Master's degree as well as a PhD in computer science from Berkeley. That he was a Unix wiz who had helped create the software language Java was an added feather in his cap as far as the recruitment team at Google were concerned. And of course it mattered that the first investors at Google (Kleiner Perkins and Sequoia Capital) were keen that Eric come on board to provide 'adult supervision' to the young and dynamic founders.

Jonathan Rosenberg, too, was not hired for his degrees in management and economics. His claim to fame was his experience with Apple and Excite, both well-known names in the tech world. After heading the immense product range at Google from 2002 onwards, Rosenberg stepped down in 2011 and later took over as COO of Motorola Mobility in 2014. He was also an advisor to Larry Page.

When Schmidt wanted to hire Sheryl Sandberg, Page and Brin were initially opposed to the idea because she was not an engineer. It is a testament to Google's incredible talent identification and development that

Sandberg not only did an amazing job at Google but later transformed Facebook into the incredible money-making machine it is today. She is credited with most of Facebook's monetization success.

Another talent at Google was Marissa Mayer, who had joined Google in 1999 as their twentieth employee and the first female one at that! She was part of Jonathan Rosenberg's team when he was heading the entire product range at Google. Being someone who has in recent years been ranked sixth on the *Fortune*'s 40 under-40 list as well as one of the 16th most powerful businesswomen in the world, Mayer is one of those Googlers who have been bred in the secret Google sauce that not only makes them the finest search engine in the world but also the top connoisseurs of talent. In 2012, Marissa Mayer took over as president and CEO of Yahoo.

It was this incessant search for talent and the ability to nurture it that led Page and team to identify another rare achiever within Googleplex. Just as Mayer was part of Rosenberg's team, this other achiever was at one time part of her unit. This was none other than Sundar Pichai. At the time of launching the Google Chrome project, Pichai was reporting to Mayer.

Google's strategy and culture has always been to get the best people on board and then give them the freedom to use their abilities without obstructing their creativity. This is one of the reasons why Pichai and others before him have delivered the goods they were supposed to deliver, time after time. And this is also one of the things that Pichai as the new CEO of Google will need to hold on to from the previous management – hire the best people, give them an eco-system that allows them to grow wings, and then get out of their way as they learn to flap their wings and soar high!

their creativity. That is one of the reasons why Pichai and others before him have delivered the goods they were supposed to deliver, time after time. And this is also one of the things that Pichai as the new CEO of Google will need to hold on to from the previous management: hire the best people, give them an eco-system that allows them to grow wings, and then get out of their way as they learn to flip their wings and soar high.

PART 4

THE PEOPLE'S LEADER

'If your actions inspire others to dream more, learn more, do more and become more, you are a leader.'

– John Quincy Adams

Nice guys can win

'Outstanding leaders go out of their way to boost the self-esteem of their personnel. If people believe in themselves, it's amazing what they can accomplish.'

– Sam Walton

In late 2014, when Sundar Pichai was elevated to heading what was virtually the entire product range at Google, it was evident to the relatively clairvoyant among us that Page was paving the way for his protégé to take over from him. In response to the move, Om Malik – a well-known venture capitalist – tweeted, 'Proof that nice guys can win.'

Yet Pichai's meteoric rise over the past decade at Google is not the victory of one man within an enterprise. It's the sum total of what the right ecosystem mixed with an appropriate dose of culture led by great men can do for other potentially great men. If the company weren't Google, and Page hadn't been the CEO leading a team of 'smart creatives', even a man with the considerable ability of Pichai might have been hard-pressed to achieve the kind of success he has.

Pichai has taken over one of the greatest companies of our time at a juncture when it faces several challenges. An average company struggles to strive. A good company strives to move ahead. But a great company like Google tries to outwit itself in order to magnify its growth quantum times. This in itself is a challenge for the IT giant. Now, there are other things that will demand the new CEO's attention. Pichai takes over a much leaner Google than the one Page left a few months ago. The challenges before the Chennai man are considerable. Some of these, if not attended to quickly, may bring an end to the magnificent spell Google has had since its inception in 1998. Unless they are nimble, a competitor could whiz past the Mountain View company.

A closer look at Google's key challenges and opportunities will give us a peek into what lies ahead.

Get the social networking story right!

'One of the tests of leadership is the ability to recognize a problem before it becomes an emergency.'

– Arnold Glasow

When it comes to Google, one expects them to do the unexpected. After all, they have a history of doing things contrarily, and more often than not it has worked in their favour. Whether it was breaking the norms of going for an IPO without depending on the investment bankers or the writing of a Warren Buffet kind of letter to prospective shareholders at the time of listing, Google has always aimed to surprise, and occasionally shock.

That is why one wonders why the gifted founders and immensely talented Googlers have not been able to break what could be called the 'social networking jinx' for the company.

Engineering versus engagement

The start wasn't too bad. While Google was not the first company to claim the social networking arena – that credit goes to Myspace – they were quick to come up with their own platform called Orkut in 2004, just a year after Myspace had launched. It's possible that Orkut, named after its creator from Google, might have quashed Myspace in years to come. Google's social networking site certainly attracted users in droves in many parts of the world, though nowhere as much as in USA, India and Brazil. But the giant that ultimately squashed Myspace was not Google but the new kid on the block – Thefacebook.com

Launched within a month of Orkut hitting the market, Zuckerberg's platform quickly overtook every other platform in the world, including the mighty Google and the pioneering Myspace. By 2008, Facebook.com (its name now changed from the earlier Thefacebook.com) had overtaken both Orkut and Myspace and was the showstopper for anything 'social'. In ensuing years other immensely popular social networking and exchange sites such as Twitter, Tumblr, Quora, Digg, Reddit, Flickr, Pinterest, Instagram, and several others have entered the fray.

Google's answer to Facebook was to slow down on Orkut and launch a second platform called Google

Friend Connect in 2008. Orkut failed for many reasons, chief among these being the fact that it was built more like a utilitarian engineering product than a youthful social platform that could create enough excitement among users to take it to scale.

Many platforms but little success

Google Friend Connect showed promise in the beginning. The fact that it helped bloggers build up followers was perhaps its biggest asset, though possibly its only one. It was shut down in March 2012, just four years from when it had been launched with great promise. The fact that many bloggers lost a significant chunk of their followers when Google shut down the platform did not endear the company to the blogging community.

Meanwhile, Google had already launched a third platform in the social networking space. This was called Google Buzz. At this juncture, observers began to wonder if Google had had a prescience that their social media was not going to work and hence they were quick to shut down the respective platforms or whether it was the fact that they were shutting down the platforms perhaps too rapidly that impacted users' perceptions. It could also be a lack of concentrated effort and focus on making one robust social networking tool that could compete with Facebook and the other players in the market. Be that as it may, Google Buzz shut down in a little more than a year. Launched in 2010, its demise was announced by the powers-that-be at Google by the end of 2011. That Google Buzz was possibly created to compete with both Facebook (social networking) and Twitter (micro blogging) ceased to matter as the plug was pulled on the third foray from Google in the social media space.

Finally, in June 2011, Google came up with its fourth version of what they felt a social networking platform should look like. The latest gladiator to hit the arena was called Google Plus. It was pitched by Google as an interest-based social networking platform. Subsequently though, the offering came to be seen as a social layer across a majority of Google services. This meant that while the Google Plus user base showed rapid upward movement, it did not translate into those users being active on the platform. The reason this was happening was that those who had signed up for some other Google service by default became Google Plus customers. However, this did not necessarily mean they would also be active users of this service. The average time spent by these users on the platform was minuscule compared to what other social networking sites reported with their user experience. Hence, while Google Plus had close to 540 million users by 2013, the average time a user spent on the site was roughly only a little more than three minutes. Users of Facebook averaged seven-and-a-half hours. The math tells its own story.

The highlight of this story is that by mid 2015 Google decided to shut down Google Plus and split it into two separate entities – photos and streams. Going by precedence and based on conjecture on how any of this is going to be different, it is difficult to guess how the latest decisions from Mountain View are going to help. Add to this the fact that platforms such as Facebook are largely closed to Google's search engine, and it's easy to see how much information Google is missing out on. As Facebook continues to grow, the amount of information Google will be unable to access off it will rise too. For a company (Google) that states its purpose is to organize all the information in the world for the user, it becomes a challenge when substantially large platforms like Facebook are off their radar.

It can be surmised while at the moment it may be just a small problem for Google that they are not in the running for the social networking race, it won't be long before it approaches an emergency-like situation for the company. This should certainly form a part of what Pichai would want to focus on in the ensuing months. The company that was able to re-imagine the manner in which people used Search seventeen years ago needs to do the same today for their social story if they want to salvage the situation.

Google's advertising supremacy – under attack?

'When it's too easy to get money, then you get a lot of noise mixed in with the real innovation and entrepreneurship. Tough times bring out the best parts of Silicon Valley.'

– Sergey Brin

In 2014, Google's revenue from advertisements was $59.06 billion. This was close to 90 per cent of the company's revenue that year. It doesn't take a genius to figure out that the cash inflows at Google are fairly skewed towards money coming through its ad engine.

It becomes quite clear just how badly the company would be affected if ad revenues were to slow down, or worse still, if the way online ads happen were to change. The worst case would be if Google is not the most disruptive player in the changed scenario and has to cede place to someone else; someone more nimble, with equally 'smart creatives' working for them and with perhaps a platform backed by greater 'technical insight' in the changed space than Google has.

Eric Schmidt and Jonathan Rosenberg (both top Googlers) have been known to talk about how important it is to have technical insight when one wants to develop a truly disruptive business idea. So, what is technical insight? Simply put, it is the underlying foundation over which the idea of a new product or a platform is overlaid. It's the basis behind applying let's say new technology to an old problem to solve it in a better manner (which was how Google itself was born) or by coming up with a singular idea that is so disruptive that it becomes a game-changer (like what InMobi is doing with mobile advertising). With the advertising game having changed over the years, Google could face challenges on various fronts.

Competition from social media players

On the one hand, social media players (led by the likes of Facebook and Twitter) have emerged as large competitors for Google for advertising. Facebook has close to a billion users, and it also has the tools to analyse this significantly sized customer data residing on their platform. The threat this poses to advertising revenue moving away from Google's coffers to the social media behemoth is not too hard to understand. Add to this the fact that most of that data is inaccessible to Google, and it magnifies the difficulties; the issue being Google's relative inability to claim a substantial share of the ad revenue from the social networking industry.

The other threat Google faces is in the videos segment – once again from Facebook. The quantum of video being watched on the social networking site has increased radically. Other players, such as Spotify and Pandora, also pose a reasonable degree of threat. While YouTube still holds a position of dominance in this segment, this could become a cause for worry in days to come unless Google does something innovative to stay differentiated.

PPC – a real issue or a perceptual problem?

The other challenge Google will face is in the pay-per-click (PPC) space where it is a market leader. Of late, the rate the company can charge advertisers when users click on a particular link has been dropping. One of the reasons could be that the CPC (cost per click) is more or less an average of the PC and mobile clicks. Since mobile clicks are relatively inexpensive (compared to desktop clicks) and the growth in desktop clicks is losing steam to the growth in mobile search, the average CPC will perhaps drop further, at least for some time.

The fact that smart phone sales have gone up significantly and that an increasing number of people use their phones for any search will only add more fuel to this fire. However, it is important to understand this phenomenon. A lot of people (including analysts) have possibly conjectured that the lower CPC bodes ill for Google. It may not really be the case.

For one thing, the CPC average has been going down because mobile clicks are cheaper. Having said that, the volume of mobile clicks has actually gone up; and therefore the reduction in CPC needs to be looked at in context of the gain in volumes in mobile clicks.

Secondly, it doesn't appear (though it is difficult to say with certainty because Google doesn't share in detail how CPC breaks down across categories) that CPC rates have declined in the more mature markets (especially USA). It is therefore quite possible that the increased volumes of Google in emerging markets (including India) may actually be leading to a lower CPC average since these markets are more price sensitive. Therefore, as long as the CPC holds in the mature markets and the overall volumes and revenue from the emerging markets is on the rise, the lower CPC rates in these areas may not be an indicator to be worried about.

Where Google may want to be careful about is how this story gets played out in the media and by extension at the stock market. There are enough precedents of stock prices plummeting, or plateauing at best, merely because the market is either irrationally exuberant or irrationally fearful. Microsoft has been through a similar situation in the past when even though revenues went up significantly during Ballmer's period as CEO, the stock price remained stagnant owing in part to a lack of strong products from the Redmond based company. To a certain extent it is also due to the way investors responded to media reports on Microsoft. The last thing Google needs in the near future is to mirror the not-so-salubrious experiences of Microsoft's past.

Is InMobi the new Google?

Sixteen years ago, Google took the world by storm because they disrupted the way search results were made available for users. Later, they were also instrumental in making advertising 'relevant' because they focused on the interest of the users rather than on which customer was willing to pay more.

Now, years later, another company called InMobi has done something similar in their space. They have used technology to disrupt the way online advertising works, and in the process have created the world's largest mobile advertising network. What makes it even more interesting is that this time the company that has the most to lose from InMobi entering the fray is none other than the challenger only 16 years ago – Google!

InMobi, which started as an Indian SMS-based search platform called mKhoj, intended to later transform into an SMS advertising network. However, by 2007 the founding team had rebranded it to the more globally recognizable name of InMobi. Their business model, too, underwent a change. While the initial funding from Mumbai Angels had been sought for the SMS-based search model, the team realized that the cultural nuances of India did not suit the plan. In a nation where almost every second person can be relied upon if one needs to seek information, MKhoj did not see traction in the early days. In a classic display of leadership decision–making, the founders decided to alter the business model. mKhoj moved to the rapidly evolving mobile web ecosystem and got rebranded as InMobi. The seed investors were supportive and after an initial period of scant funds, bigger investors like Kleiner Perkins Caufield & Byers and Sherpalo Ventures came into the picture with series A and B funding of $7.1 million and $8 million respectively. Subsequently, Softbank made an investment of more than $200 million in InMobi and things started to get exciting.

By the end of 2014, InMobi had become the most potent platform for mobile advertising in the world. Its reach extended across 200 countries and the company boasted more than a billion unique users on their network. By July 2015, InMobi took the first steps on the road to transforming advertising. They announced the launch of a 'discovery platform' that intended to change advertising into 'discovery' moments for its users. The platform was called Miip and it served to shake up the other mobile and web advertising platforms around the world. InMobi might not have been regarded as a big player thus far, but the unveiling of Miip changed all that. Facebook and Google now sat up and took notice! Rumours abounded that Google was in discussions with InMobi to buy out the latter for $1 billion. Though the rumours were largely unverified, it did establish the fact that with Miip InMobi had not-so-subtly announced its intention to disrupt mobile advertising as we know it.

One of the things that really bother smart phone users today is the increasing number of ads that are pushed on to them. The fact that these ads are even more intrusive on the small screen of the mobile makes it that much more annoying. The pet peeve users have though, is that the majority of the ads have no relevance to them. This is where Miip comes in. The revolutionary platform from InMobi is able to make sense of what a user is viewing on a mobile app, and thereon curates content and product opportunities that are relevant to the user. The fact that this is served to users in real time and in an unobtrusive manner makes it that much more interesting for them.

In turn, InMobi's advertisers are guaranteed a relevant audience. This increases the probability of success to a great degree. For the users, there is the obvious benefit of having their spoken (and occasionally unspoken) needs being addressed at the time when they are actually looking for options to satisfy the same need; all this without the accompanying disadvantage of viewing irrelevant ads.

Given the staggering number (more than one billion) of users InMobi already has on their network, Google is looking at a massive opportunity loss in terms of advertising revenue from this one player alone. Combined with the opportunity loss in advertising to Facebook (more than a billion users), the consequent cumulative loss of advertising revenue becomes a huge concern.

For Google, this means not just facing up to players like Facebook, Microsoft, Yahoo, Twitter and Millennial Media, but protecting itself from the growing influence of InMobi in the global advertising market share.

Goliath versus Goliath!

'I am not afraid of an army of lions led by a sheep; I am afraid of an army of sheep led by a lion.'

– Alexander the Great

In the past few years, there are two stories that have been spoken about and played out in most IT conferences and discussions. One of these relates to cloud services. The other is Mobile. It was only a year ago that Satya Nadella mentioned how Microsoft was readying for a 'mobile first' and 'cloud first' strategy.

The Mobile Story

Microsoft's strength in personal computing as a function of Microsoft Windows has been diluted somewhat by the burgeoning demand for mobile devices. However, the introduction of new utilities in the Windows phone 8.1 recalls some of the positive features of an iPhone and an Android phone. While Android leads the market share (it is the largest used OS in smart phones), iOS (Apple) and a transformed Microsoft (under Nadella) offer competition that possesses the capability of making the going tough for Google and its incredibly popular Android. Google would do well to pay heed to some of the advantages of the Windows phone.

While Google sold off Motorola to Lenovo, Microsoft's acquisition of Nokia gives them a distinct edge. One of this is of course the quality and design of the Windows phone. The phone has variants relevant for both the lower end of the market as well as sleek versions like the Nokia Lumia 1020. For the user, the Windows phone therefore provides great value for money. On the apps front, Android possibly offers more apps to users than Microsoft does since the Windows phone is not an open source platform like Android. Therefore, the quality of apps that Windows offers to their customers is of a far superior quality. Even the ones that are common to Android somehow look more consistent and clean on the Windows phone.

For a user, having to switch from one app to the other to perform functions or view updates is not a very satisfying experience. The Windows phone allows a better end-to-end user experience in that sense. One can view all notifications within the People Hub. Where tagging pictures is concerned, the utility makes it easier than Android. All in all, the user gets a more integrated experience with the Windows phone, something that most people value in today's age. Loyal customers of Microsoft's software breathe easier when using products like Outlook, Skype and OneDrive on the Windows phone. Also, unlike Android, a user does not have to pay for Office when using the Windows phone. One of the biggest benefits of the Windows phone over Android, however, is that it works consistently across various devices. In contrast, since Android is offered on phones that come from different manufacturers and in varying shapes and sizes, its performance and quality is sometimes questionable.

Furthermore, while Android offers a greater number of games, Windows is integrated with Xbox and offers immensely popular games, like Asphalt 8, Joyride and several more, free of cost to the user. Something that is of interest to users – especially in emerging markets where connectivity is relatively weak – is the fact that a Windows phone allows full navigation in offline mode too whereas Android phones only allow a user selective download of offline maps while driving without a connection. Additionally, the free cloud storage (in most cases up to 7 GB) and high internal storage in Windows phones diminishes the need for users to rely on third party online storage solutions. This mitigates the risk of compatibility issues.

To sum up, while Android phones certainly have the

advantage of more apps, the Windows phone offers superior integration and several other advantages. The way the market for smart phones is evolving, users worldwide will be looking for a platform that straddles across desktop, mobile and Cloud. Nadella-led Microsoft may be just the ticket to provide that heady blend and if Android does not have an answer to some of these issues, this may pose a threat to its present near-monopolistic hold over the smart phone OS market.

The threat is not just limited to the Microsoft Windows phone, which all said and done is still a distant challenger to Android. The greater threat is from Apple's iPhone which still holds sway over a large section of users and thus commands almost fanatical loyalty, the kind that makes people wait in queues on the day of the launch of a new version of the iPhone. Contemporary users of smart phones hanker after a device that is simplistic, minimalistic and gives them the freedom to run apps that they want. The iPhone does just that with its sharp focus on ease of use, quality experience and reliability.

What Pichai and Google may want to do right now is to ensure that they don't lose critical talent in this area. Amit Singhal, for instance – the man who literally rewrote the code for Google Search in 2001 – was named in 2011 by Fortune as one of the smartest people in technology. Recently, Singhal – who heads Search for Google – launched 'Now on Tap'. With this utility available on Android phones, users will be able to search more easily on their mobiles, giving subtle insights into what Google is doing to re-imagine Search on mobile. With the landscape favouring phones and apps more than desktops and websites, what Singhal and his team are doing may make a significant difference in the race for dominance in mobile.

Cloud wars

On the Cloud front, the game is slightly more complex. Things get even more complicated when one looks at different segments like IaaS, PaaS and SaaS.

SaaS (Software as a Service) makes use of the Internet to deliver third party apps whose interface is accessed on the client's end. It hosts software that a user can connect to and use. The advantage here is that a majority of SaaS applications can be run from the browser, obviating the need for downloads and installations. Since the delivery model is web-based, there is no need to install and run applications on an individual user's desktop. Furthermore, it makes it convenient for enterprises looking to simplify their maintenance and support functions since this is managed by the vendor. SaaS is more popular with consumers and the most popular uses of SaaS would therefore be email and social networking sites. Key players in the SaaS segment include the likes of Amazon, Google, Apple, Dropbox and Microsoft. Amazon rules the roost though Microsoft and Google are gradually inching forward.

PaaS (Platform as a Service) has tools that can build services of a differing nature. It layers above IaaS and enables developers to build applications on top of the computing infrastructure. For the developer community, this allows a framework upon which they can develop or customize applications. PaaS is very popular with developers because it does away with the need for them to manage and execute, leaving that to the service provider. The developer is therefore free to focus on app development.

IaaS (Infrastructure as a Service) on the other hand is more popular among users into high computing areas and research. It is the foundational layer in cloud services and deals with VMs (virtual machines), storage (hard disks), servers and network among other things. The computing resources and storage offered by IaaS helps developers and companies deliver business solutions.

While price has played a major role in the 'cloud wars' until now, it is felt that price alone may not be the differentiating factor in the near future. The game going forward will be more of integration and offering advanced features. As of now, Amazon is the clear market leader in the $16 billion cloud market, Microsoft is a distant second and IBM and Google bring up the third and fourth positions respectively.

While Dropbox is considered a pioneer in cloud services, among the larger players Amazon is labelled the 'thought leader' at least in the IaaS space. Amazon Web Services (AWS) have more than five times the computing capacity as compared to the other top 14 players in this space. Their ability to provide innovative services and monitoring tools has also been a point in favour of Amazon. And in a market driven to a great extent by prices, Amazon (along with Google) has demonstrated a consistent ability and willingness to offer the most competitive rates.

Microsoft's Azure on the other hand, has exhibited the highest year on year growth in the IaaS space. The fact that Azure's admin tools are extremely easy to use (even more so for Windows administrators) makes it an attractive choice. Moreover, it is similar to AWS in the sense that its IaaS can also be used as a PaaS. On the pricing front, Nadella at Microsoft has demonstrated commitment to matching price cuts from competitors like AWS and Google. And for Microsoft's enterprise customers it is an added sweetener that Microsoft offers them a discounted rate for Azure cloud computing services. Given that Nadella is largely seen as the man behind Azure, if he can ensure that Microsoft's cloud services have clear differentiators, it will enable them to gain higher visibility in an increasingly cluttered market. The enterprise business in any case has always been a strength for Microsoft and this is the area that competitors like Google need to break into if they hope to garner a larger share of the pie.

IBM's offerings on cloud computing have been a major contributor in the hybrid and private cloud market. While it is the third largest in market share of IaaS, it is second to Microsoft as far as year on year growth is concerned. Their well considered investment in SoftLayer has further given an impetus to their growth in this market. Probably the biggest factor in IBM's favour is that 50 per cent of their strategic outsourcing customers, who are also among the largest enterprises globally, are implementing cloud computing solutions with IBM.

Google has been investing big time in cloud computing. Its service offerings are also being ramped up rapidly. Google has also exhibited strong focus on matching Amazon for every price cut the latter has made. The fact that Google charges by the minute (with a minimum usage of ten minutes) is a big benefit for small businesses given that AWS charges by the hour. However, while Google cloud platform's down time is much better than that of Azure (Microsoft), it is still not as reliable as Amazon's. While Google is clearly doing well in SaaS, and it has made efforts on the enterprise side, its services have historically been more consumer-oriented than corporate. This will certainly not make it easy for data centre managers using the Google cloud platform unless Google makes some tangible changes in this area.

What Google may want to do (and is probably doing already to a degree) is endeavour to offer a strong alternative to Windows on the desktop and mobile through Chrome OS and Android. This would go a long way in providing Google control of the standard app space and revenue from the software side. While Amazon would still lead the IaaS space, Google would leverage strengths on the SaaS side. Alternatively, Google could take a leaf out of IBM's book and have parallel focus on capturing the higher end of the market by developing cognitive computing platforms. While the other cloud services may be more price sensitive, the higher end of the value chain may be a little more immune to price wars. In short, Google would do well to follow a three-pronged approach – consolidate its position in the consumer-oriented cloud services; balance price cuts with a platform-service-features approach; and focus on developing cognitive computing platforms for the upper end of the value chain.

Leading without a title!

'Great leaders are almost always great simplifiers, who can cut through argument, debate and doubt to offer a solution everybody can understand.'

– General Colin Powell

Some people are chosen to lead while there are those who expend great efforts to be placed in leadership roles. There are a rare few who grow into leadership even before they are formally given that title. Sundar Pichai belongs to the latter tribe.

Without exception, those who have had the opportunity to work alongside Pichai classify him as someone who is not just incredibly intelligent but also extraordinarily collaborative and empathic. This in itself is good enough to slide into potential leadership. However, Pichai takes collaboration a step further. Even when he was not the CEO, he had a terrific knack for understanding what Larry Page (CEO at the time) wanted to communicate to others in the organization. In fact, Page has been known to say that Pichai is often able to explain his thoughts even better than he can!

Colleagues at Google narrate a story about Pichai that exemplifies this trait rather well. In a meeting that Page addressed with a group of vice presidents and directors across product categories, he spoke about various concepts and introduced several ideas. A lot of what he said didn't quite connect with areas that the team gathered there was expecting. Consequently, when Page brought the meeting to a close and walked out of the room, his exit was greeted with complete silence. At this stage, Pichai walked in and explained to the gathering what he thought Page meant. Not content with doing that, he followed it up by meeting the various teams separately and helping them think about how to move ahead on the various projects in a cohesive manner. What Pichai did that day went beyond mere collaboration or articulation of a manager's thought process. He acted as a leader would, seizing ownership of what needed to be done and ensuring that everyone concerned understood what each one of them was required to do. He did not wait for Page to confer a title on him before he felt comfortable doing what he did. At the same time, this and various other occasions persuaded Page that Pichai was someone who could not just rephrase what he wanted to say, but that he would also take ownership and lead the way on critical projects.

There are those who are concerned about the flight of senior leadership from Google in the wake of Pichai's ascension. The reasoning behind this is that Pichai has been promoted over several people who at one time were significantly senior to him, and a few people among this group may not be happy working in a Google where Pichai is now CEO. While this does not seem to be a logical enough reason for senior Googlers exiting the company, theorists cite examples of a few veterans who have left the organization in recent years. Andy Rubin (co-founder of Android), for instance, stepped down as head of Android in March 2013 when Page handed over to Pichai. At that time Page had said that Rubin would be managing the robotics division at Google. However, in October 2014, Rubin resigned from Google. The timing of his resignation came close on the heels of Pichai being named overall head of products at Google, even though Pichai's elevation had nothing to do with the division Rubin was involved in. A few months later (March 2015), another veteran at Google – Alan Eustace – quit the company. Eustace had worked as SVP of engineering and later as SVP for the knowledge division. Eustace did not pick up a role at another company and nor did he start his own venture like Andy Rubin had after leaving Google. Vivek Gundotra, who was SVP for social at Google resigned in April 2014, though his move at least doesn't seem to have been remotely connected to Pichai's elevation, either in 2014 (SVP for products) or 2015 (CEO of Google). Sebastian Thrun – a key contributor to the Google X project – stepped down from his role at Google in September 2014 though his move was possibly owing to a desire to focus on his education startup, Udacity.

The fact remains that Google has lost a fair share of talent in recent years. A considerable share left for Facebook and other exciting startups that promised big valuations and disruptive business models. Some have left owing to management-driven re-organizations and some due to personal decisions. A fair share of the exits have been at the top, where it has hit Google the most, especially when it needs its best and most experienced talent.

Sundar Pichai's strengths in managing people and their expectations may come in handy at this juncture. On the one hand he will need to create opportunities for budding talent within strategic roles to retain them, and on the other he will need to manage the dissonance (if indeed it exists) of former veterans at Google who may be having trouble seeing him in the CEO's seat.

Pichai has already begun to pick up high quality, high EQ talent and placing them in key roles. Hiroshi Lockheimer's appointment to head Android is a case in point. Lockheimer mirrors Pichai in that his engineering skills are matched by his people oriented. His style of managing is different from the way Rubin and his associates (Hugo Barra and Steve Horowitz) managed Android. And this might be just what the company needs at the moment. The other person Pichai has recently incorporated into the team to handle a key function – as SVP for sales and operations – is Philipp Schindler. Schindler has the sales panache of his former boss – the legendary Nikesh Arora – and the relationship-management skills that seem to be modelled on Pichai's own style. If one were to go by these two appointments, Pichai's view of Google seems quite clear; he intends it to be a company led by people who have the capability of balancing both their tasks and people-orientation.

As long as Pichai can keep his key resources within the company, Google is not just safe but well-poised to take on competition and respond to a rapidly changing technology landscape.

Don't be evil!

'We have tried to define precisely what it means to be a force for good – always do the right, ethical thing. Ultimately, "Don't be evil" seems the easiest way to summarize it.'

– Sergey Brin

Stacy Sullivan joined Google as the head of human resources in 2000. A year later she was holding court in a room with a bunch of other people at Google, in a classic attempt to draw out a list of corporate values that Googlers could abide by. What started with bromides like 'Google will strive to honour all its commitments' was brought to a sudden halt when one of the people present – Paul Buchheit – blurted out what he thought ought to define the cultural values at Google. The words 'Don't be evil' resounded around the room like a joke. And that was exactly what the people present thought at first! Engineer Paul Buccheit had cracked a funny one. The only two people who didn't quite agree were the man who had made the proposal (Paul), and Stacy, who was trying to nail down a set of corporate values that sounded lofty enough for people to live by. Buccheit, who had previously worked at Intel, was cynical about value themes that sounded like platitudes and felt his suggestion summed up the culture a startup ought to have. Stacy Sullivan on the other hand didn't see it the same way at first and felt that the 'Don't be evil' slogan didn't quite measure up to what Google would want to embed as part of its culture. Sullivan had the support of early hires like Marissa Mayer and Salar Kamangar. But Buchheit was insistent. Somewhere at the back of his mind there was a strong feeling that Google shouldn't be like Microsoft, which in those days was going through challenges of being monopolistic and ruthless with competition, unwittingly earning the moniker of 'evil' from a lot of quarters.

What started off being construed as a joke was finally accepted when Sullivan and others realized Buchheit wasn't going to back down. And that has been the defining theme that Google has endeavoured to live by since. This, however, has attracted a lot of criticism from people who feel that Google has somewhat moved away from the idealistic motto it set for itself.

One major front of criticism relates to privacy issues. As mentioned earlier in the book, it started with Gmail and the apprehension that Google was wantonly invading people's personal zones in the way the company had aligned ads to email content. While this was later addressed in part by Google, it was the first time Google's image changed from that of an innocent, fun-loving startup to something a little more intimaditing. Google Buzz was next in line for criticism, again on trust issues. This invited the ire of the Federal Trade Commission. The company's efforts to digitize all the books in the world was met with strong dissent from authors and publishers, though in this case there might actually have been a load of good as books around the world would be accessible to everyone. However, it was deemed that the project would grant Google virtual monopoly. In another case, the Google Street View feature was met with considerable resistance because it appeared to violate privacy on various grounds. Google eventually responded by blurring images and employing other means, but the resultant views were not of high quality and the damage to Google's image on the privacy issue had in any case deepened further. In yet another instance, Google's face recognition app (Goggles) was expected to encourage stalking and was likewise slammed.

More recently, the European Commission charged Google with skewing their search results. It suggested that Google was doing this to favour its comparison shopping service. It was also concerned that the company was promoting proprietary services like Google maps and Google Search on the Android mobile OS, shutting out rivals in the process. In August

2015, the Competition Commission of India (CCI) accused Google of abusing its dominant position to manipulate search outcomes. This included search results as well as sponsored links that are displayed on the right hand side of the search results page. CCI's move was the first instance globally of an antitrust body making a formal charge against Google and it was based on responses from 30 businesses including e-commerce, travel, social media and search, among others. Some of the well-known companies that were part of this included Flipkart, MakeMyTrip.com, Microsoft and Facebook.

While the latest charges against Google are still under consideration, there is no doubt that Google's image in recent years has undergone substantial erosion on the aspects of trust, privacy and fairness. The 'Don't be evil' company is under attack for doing just that – being evil. And the tag will stick longer unless Google and Sundar Pichai take definite steps to address causal factors, including increased and transparent communication with various stakeholders, especially those that made Google what it is today – the millions of users!

Taming the Dragon

'Oh, East is East and West is West, and never the twain shall meet, till earth and sky stand presently at God's great judgment seat; but there is neither East nor West, border, nor breed, nor birth, when two strong men stand face to face, though they come from the ends of the earth!'

– Rudyard Kipling

In the past, various organizations from different parts of the Western world have endeavoured to enter the Chinese market. The latter represents a mammoth market with the world's largest population and millions of users on the Internet. It is also the destination that veteran companies like Dell have claimed is their second-largest market after the USA. No surprise then that a majority of the companies have changed tack or adapted themselves when it comes to the question of doing business with the dragon. Google hasn't!

China vs. Google – Round One

Yahoo was one of the first Internet companies from the West to enter China. Microsoft was the other big player. Google's approach to the Chinese market was relatively different. At first they did not set up an office in China, opting instead to focus on the market through their US office. They did, however, do it differently from Yahoo. The engineers at Google created a version of the search engine that would recognize character-based Asian languages like Mandarin. By early 2001, if a user in China looked up Google.com, Google's servers would automatically divert the user to the Chinese language search interface. This worked like a breeze. In two years, Google owned 25 per cent market share for Search in China. Unlike Baidu, whose focus was more on young users looking for MP3 downloads, Google set their sights on the white-collar urban working-class folks in the larger cities of China.

Just when it looked like things couldn't go wrong for Google, the site disappeared. Users in China were unable to access Google.com. While there was speculation that competitors of Google in China, including Baidu, might have helped persuade the Chinese government that Google was detrimental to Chinese interests, the rumour was never really proven. However, Baidu, which had a 3 per cent market share of Search in 2002 compared to 24 per cent of Google, saw its fortunes change rapidly as Google became a no-option for users in China.

Google was unblocked after a few weeks. However, China's 'firewall' was slowing down the site. Google found itself between a rock and a hard place. If they continued to operate in China from the USA, the site would be abysmally slow and in several instances users would simply migrate to Baidu and other local search engines. If on the other hand, they were to set up business in China, having an office on Chinese soil meant being subject to all of China's laws, including censorship regulations. Google decided that it made more sense to take the latter approach. The way they saw it, while they would need to censor a percentage of search results in China, they would at least be contributing by improving access to information on various other counts. By the end of 2005, Google had signed documents that allowed them to operate an Internet service in China.

In January 2006, Google launched the search engine for China. Now, Google had two sites operational for users in China. One was Google.com, which was uncensored but sluggish because of the firewall. The other was Google.cn, which on the first day of operation was flooded with people (especially human rights activists) wanting to check it out who, to their chagrin, found that the invisible hand of censorship was absolute on the site.

Google succumbing to the demands of censorship in China got them the brunt of negative public opinion in the USA, as people saw them moving away from the 'Don't be evil' motto. But that was only part of the trouble. The Redmond-based company had to defend itself in front of the Committee on International Relations of the US House of Representatives. While they were not alone in this – Microsoft, Yahoo and Cisco Systems were also under attack by legislators – Google surprisingly had to bear the brunt of the indignation as they were questioned on how a company with their motto ended up agreeing to censorship in China.

On the subject of pressuring China to ease up on censorship, while visiting China to meet Kai-Fu Lee, Eric Schmidt (then CEO of Google) told journalists, 'I think it is arrogant for us to walk into a country where we are just beginning operations and tell that country how to run itself.'

Whatever be the case, the events of Google acquiescing to China's censorship laws, and the consequent public outrage in the USA followed by the stance taken by the US legislators, lent Google the perception of being in a curiously tenuous state.

Round Two – and Knock Out

By 2005, Google had grown in size and the number of people they employed had shot up, too. New offices had been set up across the globe. Schmidt and Page figured it was time to enter the market that defied all other markets in terms of sheer size and consumer demand – China!

At this juncture, Google already had the majority share of the search market in China, without even having a physical presence there. Schmidt and team decided to hire a man called Kai-Fu Lee. Lee had the perfect credentials to help Google succeed in their China endeavours. There was only one problem. Lee was Microsoft's key man in China!

Among his various contributions to Microsoft, Kai-Fu Lee had set up Microsoft Research Asia in Beijing. Lee knew about Google's intended foray into China. Discussions began between him and the Google leadership team that resulted in him being offered the role of president for Google Greater China. Microsoft, unwilling to concede another resource to Google – this time one of their key people – cautioned Lee against jumping ship. But Lee had set his heart on the younger company, and Google wasn't playing hard-to-get either. The offer was made and Microsoft dragged Lee and Google to court.

By December 2005, the legal issues on Kai-Fu Lee's joining Google had been sorted out with Microsoft, and Microsoft's erstwhile head honcho in China became Google's critical employee there. The timing couldn't have been better. Yahoo had invested $1 billion in a fast-growing company called Alibaba in China. Baidu – China's answer to Google in Search – had gone public in August earlier that year and its stock price was soaring. Search and advertising were growing exponentially as businesses. And Google figured it was time to expand to the largest market in the world. The fact that a foothold in China would also make them visible to the thousands of computer scientists graduating from Chinese universities was the icing on the cake. Consequently, by January 2006, Google had set up shop in China. In the next two years, Google had increased their market share in Search from 19.2 per cent to 22.8 per cent. Baidu, on the other hand, saw a decline in their share from 63.7 per cent to 58.1 per cent. However, Google still remained number two to Baidu. Till 2009, traffic to Google.cn grew and revenues soared.

And then things started to go wrong.

In December 2009 Google noticed that their site was being targeted by hackers. A rapidly assembled team led by Sergey Brin found out where the hacking was emanating from. It left them stupefied! The hacking activity originated from outside China. Once again, Google did the unprecedented. They publicly shared details about the hacking activity on their site. A public announcement was made soon thereafter that Google would no longer be censoring search results on Google.cn.

This was followed by discussions with officials in China. Google maintained their public stance of delivering uncensored search results and the China government was not willing to back down on their censorship laws. It was no surprise then that by March 2010, Google.cn was shut down. And since then, Google.com has faced severe blockage by the Chinese firewall, resulting in steep drops in traffic.

The question here is – could Google have handled this differently? No reasoning would be entirely right or wrong. On one side there is the law of the land and on the other the desire to encourage freedom of expression. While it may appear that the twain can never meet, that may not necessarily be true.

In the aftermath of Google walking out of China, people at Googleplex may have felt more respect for the leadership team but nothing changed for the better in China. Motorola dropped Google for Search in China in favour of Baidu and Bing. Dell and HP continued to focus on the China market. Microsoft and Yahoo did not seem keen to emulate Google's decision, either. The loser in the bargain was the user in China who now would not only be deprived of uncensored results, but would also not have access to any search information whatsoever from the largest search engine in the world. The adverse impact this logically has on freedom of information in China is interestingly the opposite of what Google might have been thinking of when they decided to move out of the market. Of course for Google, moving out of China was tantamount to not being able to address the information needs of one-fifth of the world's population!

What Google should have considered – Guanxi

More businesses than can be covered in this volume have lost their footing or run afoul of local laws when they fail to understand the cultural nuances of the market they venture into with such enthusiasm. It appears that Google unwittingly made the same mistake.

In China, understanding the concept of Guanxi is critical.

What is 'Guanxi?'

It is concerned with the advantages one may gain from social connections. If one were to explain this in a very rudimentary manner, it would be the equivalent of what 'social networking' is in the western parts of the world. The Chinese deem it important to develop a host of Guanxi relationships that span both their personal and business lives. The concept of 'reciprocity' is very significant in this process. This means that if I ask you for a favour, I have automatically set myself up to return that favour. Not returning the favour, even if asked for it at a much later date, would be construed a grave offence in China.

Guanxi is an important concept to understand when one is doing business in China because business interactions there are not separate from the social ones. If anything, the former is deeply layered into the latter. Hence, Guanxi operates at two levels. One, in the connections that are made with business stakeholders – competition, suppliers, manufacturers, vendors, etc. The other is the relationship with government officials and regulatory authorities. Guanxi, therefore, plays a defining role in its influencing power over business success for any company that plans to operate in China.

This is especially true for China where Guanxi is literally embedded in the country's culture as it enables the fostering of relationships between businesses, and between businesses and government. Google did a great job of managing the first part, that is, the stakeholder relationships between them and other businesses. They established partnerships with China Mobile, Xunlei and China Telecom. China Mobile was the dominant mobile phone carrier in China that assisted in managing Google's mobile Internet search services. Xunlei was similar to YouTube and is a music and video-sharing site in China. China Telecom is one of the largest wireless telecom and broadband services provider in the world. The strategic partnership with Tianya.com (an online community) was also done beautifully as most Chinese prefer chats and online communities to writing mails or sending texts. However, Google ended up ignoring the other equally (if not more) important component of Guanxi – relationships with the government and regulatory authorities. This hit them hard!

At the core of all this is perhaps the lack of understanding of cultural nuances prevalent in China. An underlying element of Guanxi is 'saving face'. The moment Google went public with the hacking incident and their decision to serve uncensored results on Google.cn, they unwittingly made China lose face in front of the world. For the Chinese, this was unpardonable!

If Google had discussed the situation with China, there was at least a possibility of things working out; if not entirely what either party wanted, perhaps a middle ground could have been reached. As things stood, officials in China were fuming, and Google was left holding the ashes from the demise of years of effort invested in China, and the loss of more than three hundred million users.

This is one place where Google could have taken a leaf out of Microsoft's book. Notwithstanding some lapses from Microsoft where user information has been compromised, the company has made efforts to adapt to China's environment rather than try and change it. They rethought their strategy in the light of how they understood the culture in the market. Huge investments were made in China without making profits but fostering cooperation projects. Microsoft adopted Guanxi – give in order to take – and while it has been a long road for the company, what lies ahead looks more promising for the effort.

The dragon it seems cannot be tamed; but he might be open to being understood!

Don't look for faster horses!

'Never tell people how to do things.
Tell them what to do and they will surprise you
with their ingenuity.'

– General George Patton

For a company that disrupted the way Search was used all over the world, it's disappointing and surprising when people say that Google may have lost the Midas touch that comes with cutting-edge innovation.

Steve Ballmer (of Microsoft) once called Google 'a

one-trick pony', referring to Google's skewed reliance on search-related advertising for revenue. This was in stark contrast to what Steve Jobs (Apple) said to Page: 'You guys are doing too much stuff.' However, if one looks closely, both things may be pointing to the same potential issue – the absence of innovation. Doing too much might lead the company to come up with several products without being able to innovate around a few really disruptive ones. And Ballmer's jibe of Google being a one-trick pony may be reflective of the absence of a disruptive technology emanating out of Google's own labs after their search engine.

While the Google search engine was a game-changer, and later Chrome was truly innovative, the fact is that Google has acquired more innovative products than it has invented within the walls of Googleplex in recent years. YouTube was acquired, while a similar product from Google's stable wasn't as successful. Picasa (photo management) and DoubleClick (Web ads) were also acquired. As were Keyhole (later Google Earth) and Urchin for web analytics (subsequently branded as Google Analytics). Even Android, now the mobile bet for Google, was acquired from Andy Rubin and his co-founders. While all of these were amazing products, and Google showed gumption in making the acquisitions, the fact is that the majority of innovations or creative products one sees at Google lately have been incubated elsewhere. This is thought-provoking given that Google houses some of the brightest engineers in the world and in general the leadership there places great store by innovation.

It cannot be that Google is scared of failure. Larry Page has been known to compliment engineers in the past for 'failing' even when millions of dollars have been lost in the bargain. The fact that Google invested in products like Google Video, Buzz, Orkut, Google+, Google Answers, Google Notebook (later Google Docs), Google Wave, Google Health and scores of others that didn't make the cut implies that the company has not been shy of trying out different things. The idea of fast-tracking failure in order to eventually produce large value success stories is something the Google team has believed in all along.

The answer possibly lies in analysing some of their failures and a few of their successes. Google Search was immensely successful not because Google was trying to emulate Yahoo or the other older players in Search. They weren't trying to 'build a faster horse'. They were attempting to solve a problem they saw the world facing and, as Henry Ford would have put it, in the process instead of looking for a faster horse they just reinvented the whole carriage. The result was a superior search engine that was truly disruptive. While creating Chrome, they were not trying to duplicate or mirror Internet Explorer or Firefox. They were yet again trying to solve a problem in a different way. The result this time was a browser that changed the paradigm and saw Internet Explorer nose-diving while Chrome ate away at its market share.

Then, it seems the lines got blurred between trying to solve the world's problems and focusing on Google's own problems. The focus moved from finding solutions for problems to trying to combat threats from competitors like Facebook. Trying to gain a foothold in the social networking space seems to have consumed the Search giant and products were rolled out only to shut down thereafter in quick succession.

Why did these products not work out? Perhaps Google was trying to create a product while social media and networking isn't about the product. It is about what the product means for the people who are going to use it! And here Google seems to have faltered. Orkut was more of a utility product – something out of an engineer's mind – rather than one that facilitated engagement or excitement among young users. Buzz had its own issues on privacy. And while Google+ succeeded in adding people from different Google services to it, it failed to get them to do what they were supposed to on a social network.

Additionally, a company is only as innovative as the people it employs. Google's startup culture was summed up in the original founder's letter Page and Brin wrote, 'Google is not a conventional company. We do not intend to become one.' The startup culture survived way beyond the initial few years, and talent was attracted to the company because of visions and dreams of building something disruptive. Somewhere down the line, while the intent to be unconventional has remained, the focus seems to have shifted somewhere else. While Google still attracts great talent, the really creative ones seem to be headed to younger and more nimble organizations. And it's not just Facebook that has been the destination for the highly charged and creatively oriented talent. Other just-out-of-the-shell startups have also garnered a fair share of such people. In fact, Google seems to be losing out on the war for talent to companies that are perhaps seen as the 'old Google'.

It's not just about attracting creative talent. It's as much a challenge to retain the really innovative folks at Googleplex. The company has lost key talent in the past few years. Some of these examples have been shared earlier in the book. However, a case in point is that of Kevin Systrom. Google has what is known as the Associate Product Manager (APM) programme. This owes its origin to Marissa Mayer (currently

CEO of Yahoo) who at that point was reporting to Jonathan Rosenberg, then SVP and head of products at Google. The APM programme was designed, among other things, to recruit the brightest of the bright talent in computer science from colleges. Kevin Systrom's talent was recognized by veteran Googler Salar Kamangar who recommended that Systrom be inducted into the prestigious APM programme. Systrom did not have a degree in computer science and so this did not happen. Systrom left Google and cofounded his own company. Today, that company is known as Instagram. Systrom sold his company to Facebook in 2012 for $1 billion.

Evan Williams was another ex-Googler, and he cofounded Twitter in 2006. His former venture (Blogger) was sold to Google in 2003 before he joined the company. Paul Buchheit, one of the key people behind Gmail and the man who came up with the motto 'Don't be evil', left Google to start FriendFeed, which was subsequently acquired by Facebook. Another senior Googler, David Rosenblatt founded DoubleClick, which was acquired by Google. The immensely popular Pinterest site was created by Ben Silbermann who earlier worked at Google as a product designer. Dave Girouard from Google launched Upstart, and two other Googlers – Jonathan Wall and Marc Freed Finnegan – came up with Tappmo.

Howcast was launched by yet another Googler, Jason Liebman.

According to another ex-Googler, James Whittaker, 'Google's focus on Social and advertising is killing entrepreneurship and innovation.' While this may not be entirely true, the fact remains that in recent years Google has not only seen a flight of talent but has also found it increasingly difficult to compete with nimbler and more exciting startups in the battle to hire the right people.

The lack of innovation in recent times could be one of the reasons why Larry Page decided to form Alphabet as the holding company. The plan is to have Google focus on core Internet-related businesses while Alphabet will dwell on far-out projects like Calico, Life Sciences, Project Loon and various other moon shots. Hopefully the new structure will encourage greater innovation, not just at the other businesses in Alphabet but also within the one business that is still the largest within the new structure – Google!

PART 5

THE RAINMAKER

'A leader takes people where they want to go. A great leader takes people where they don't necessarily want to go, but ought to be.'

– Rosalynn Carter

Getting back to the core

'Which is why I do want Google to see, push, and invest more in making sure computing is more accessible, connectivity is more accessible. And going back to our core mission, when we do things like machine learning and assist users, I view that as a huge game-changer. Because, over time, someone who has access to just a smart phone hopefully has the same capabilities

as someone who is more privileged. That's what's very exciting about what we are doing.'

– Sundar Pichai

A lot has been said in the preceding pages about the founders' vision for Google and how sticking to that vision for the better part of the company's lifetime has helped make Google one of the most respected companies in the world. However, there are those who feel that somewhere along the way the company has lost sight of its dedicated aim to change the world through information and instead got entangled with trappings that are synonymous with the kind of conventional companies that Google's founders spoke against in their original founders' letter. However, with Sundar Pichai taking over as CEO and reiterating his commitment to Google's original lofty ideals, things seem to be back on track for the company.

If anyone can get together the vast resources of Google and convert them into a series of well-thought-through innovative bets, it has to be Pichai. With his proven knack of launching winning products, Google stands a chance of not just being counted among the most valued companies but also regaining its former glory as one of the most innovative companies in the world. Not being focused merely on product but also on technology that has the ability to change people's lives everywhere, Pichai simply needs to focus on Google's product vision and research projects. As in the early days of Google – if the users get what they truly want, they will give back to Google what the company needs most – a loyal and unlimited base of users for its wide array of services. And that is the law of Guanxi – 'before you take, you must give.'

Leading by not leading

'I start with the premise that the function of leadership is to produce more leaders, not more followers.'

– Ralph Nader

Larry Page and Sergey Brin have on countless occasions demonstrated what happens when you give a creative and driven mind the environment to lead. Sundar Pichai is a product of that environment. As were Marissa Mayer, Jonathan Rosenberg, Sheryl Sandberg, Salar Kamangar and scores of other leaders. With the formation of Alphabet, Page has in essence compelled himself and the other members of the team to walk into leadership. While Pichai takes over at Google, there are others who are priming themselves to lead the other divisions under Alphabet. Page and Brin have gone back to doing what they do best: take a larger view of things while exceedingly capable followers ready themselves to lead. This ensures that Google and the other businesses under Alphabet stay focused on laying small strategic bets that return big dividends in the future. Page and Brin are far away enough from the business to see the larger picture but not too far to miss it completely.

Also, with the more far-out projects now removed from Google's operations, the founders will be compelled to look at blending pragmatism with some of their ambitious projects, thereby bringing some method to the deliberate madness. At the same time, not having to keep an eye on the non-core business of Google will force Pichai and team to search for innovation within the core of what Google does.

Eyeing the future

'Lots of companies don't succeed over time. What do they fundamentally do wrong? They usually miss the future.'

– Larry Page

Pichai has the rather onerous task of proving to naysayers why Google should still be considered an unconventional company when by most standards it seems to have become a conventional one. If that sounds rough, then it most likely is. But at present, 85 per cent or more of the company's revenue still comes from advertising. In that sense, isn't Google just like a conventional media company? With so much reliance on advertising – and most of it online – Google needs to consider the risk of shifts in advertising behaviour that could impact their business model adversely. Or the risk that some day another innovative tech geek just might create a disruptive technology that changes the paradigm completely; technology that doesn't require the Internet or the mobile to either share information or serve advertisements. If that were to happen, Google may cease to exist as we know it today. Pichai has the unenviable job of not just keeping the company ahead of visible competitors but also looking ahead to predict trends and adapt to it before the change happens.

Final words to the wise

> *'Francois Rabelais. He was a poet. And his last words were, "I go to seek a Great Perhaps." That's why I'm going. So I don't have to wait until I die to start seeking a Great Perhaps.'*
>
> – John Green

Pichai inherits from his former mentor and CEO, Larry Page, a Google that can still boast of being among the most valuable companies across the globe with cash reserves that run into billions of dollars. There is a sound mobile strategy and Android still has the largest market share in mobile OS. While Amazon, Microsoft and IBM lead the Cloud game, Google is not too far behind, at least compared to the latter two. In Search it still rules the roost, though Bing and Yahoo are pounding close at its heels. The mobile advertising and discovery platform is where it could get really tricky with players like InMobi and Millennial Media innovating in that space. On all other products too, as of now it is holding its own with a place in one of the top five slots for each category.

The real challenge for Pichai is not just maintaining the legacy he inherits from Page but in taking each of Google's products and platforms to scale, and in Google's context that would mean something really large.

While areas like Search, Cloud and Mobile definitely need a lot of thinking from the new CEO of Google, Pichai's mind share must be spent in thinking about that which has not yet happened – thinking about the 'Great Perhaps', for within its fold may lie the kernel of innovation and disruptive creativity required to re-energize Google.

NOTES

1 *A Handbook on University System*, R. Ponnusamy & J. Pandurangan, Chennai: Allied Publishers Pvt. Ltd., 2014

2 'Meet Google's new Android chief Sundar Pichai': www.goanvoice.ca, Prof. Sanat Roy, IIT Kharagpur, 2013

3 'Chennai's Sundar Pichai is dark horse': www.timesofindia.com, Ishan Srivastava & Hemali Chhapia, 2014

4 'Fading American dream: Sundar Pichai is a metaphor for a new kind of elitism in US', Wajahat Qazi, www.firstpost.com, 2015

5 'Google drops an email bomb': www.bloomberg.com, Alex Salkever, 2004

6 'Chrome SVP Sundar Pichai Confirms Chrome Is (Mostly) Beating IE': SarahPerez, www.techcrunch.com, 2012

ALSO AVAILABLE FROM HACHETTE INDIA

An insightful account of Satya Nadella the man and the professional

The appointment of Satya Nadella, the man from Hyderabad, as CEO of Microsoft Corp. in 2014 sent waves of curiosity, speculation and expectation through the tech world at home and abroad.

What drives the man chosen to lead tech giant Microsoft into the future? What does Nadella's appointment herald for Microsoft and, indeed, for the tech industry as a whole? And will Satya Nadella be able to reinvent and re-imagine the company that once captured the imagination of every techie and customer in the world?

Addressing these questions through reportage and incisive analysis, *Nadella: The Changing Face of Microsoft* is an engaging and informative account of the most-watched man in the IT business arena and the company he leads. It will enlighten as much as it will inspire.

For further details and information, please visit www.hachetteindia.com

HACHETTE INDIA

Bestselling Business Books

THE ELEPHANT CATCHERS

THE 80/20 MANAGER

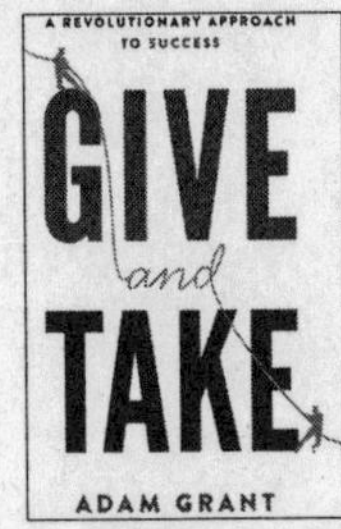

GIVE AND TAKE

COLD STEEL

THE 10-DAY MBA

FISH

STEVE JOBS

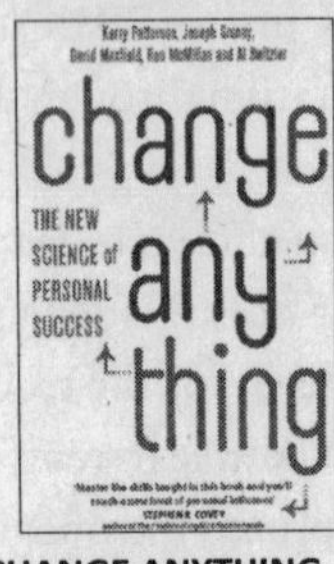

CHANGE ANYTHING

18 MINUTES

JACK, STRAIGHT FROM THE GUT

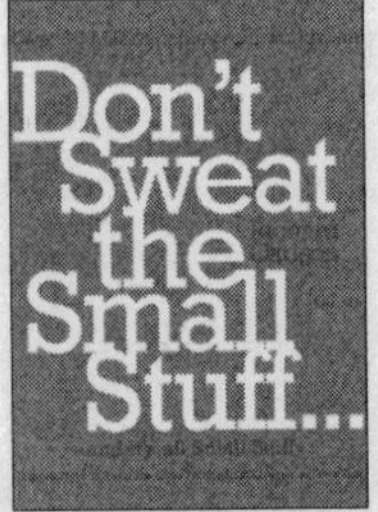

DON'T SWEAT THE SMALL STUFF

15 INVALUABLE LAWS OF GROWTH

HACHETTE INDIA

Bestselling Non-fiction Books

BIG DATA

NOW FOR THEN

THE NEW DIGITAL AGE

THE TIPPING POINT

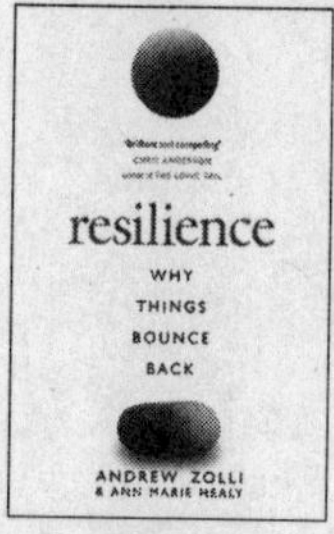

RESILIENCE

ADAPT

THE UNDERCOVER ECONOMIST

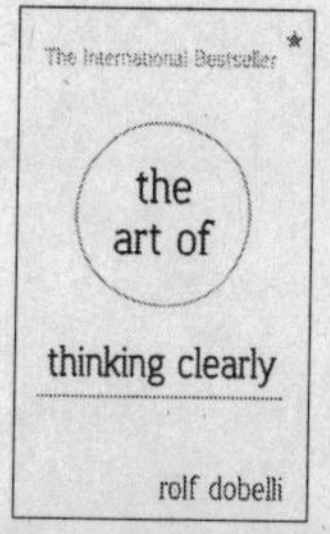

THE ART OF THINKING CLEARLY

THE ART OF CHOOSING